Praise f
Year of Y

"Rhimes is a natural storyteller. The tiniest epiphanies feel like revelations in her hands."

—*New York Times Book Review*

"Revealing and delightful."

—*New York Daily News*

"There's real value in the experiences Rhimes shares. . . . When, for example, she discusses learning to take better care of herself, the memoir feels honest, raw and revelatory."

—*Washington Post*

"*Year of Yes* is as fun to read as Rhimes's TV series are to watch. Her authorial voice is fresh and strong."

—*Los Angeles Times*

"Instead of writing passionate narratives for her TV characters, Rhimes adopted their pluck and bold attitudes and attacked life with a new sense of purpose. . . . Who knew that such a small word could have such a life-changing impact? By saying yes, she learned to dance it out and stand in the sun. Dr. Cristina Yang would be so proud."

—*Associated Press*

"Rhimes's humor and irreverence resonates as she shares what it's like to lose more than a hundred pounds, survive the 'Mommy Wars,' give speeches and even make her acting debut. Having this book nearby is like having your own Cristina Yang (Rhimes's favorite best friend TV character) on call."

—*Chicago Tribune*

"Chatty, fast-paced, smart, funny, candid and profound, reminiscent of the intelligent humor and astute observations of Nora Ephron and Roxane Gay. The year Rhimes spent saying yes to everything changed her life, and though her book isn't prescriptive, it just might change yours."

—*Los Angeles Daily News*

"Rhimes is, unsurprisingly, a fantastic memoirist: her writing is conversational and witty and lyrical, inflected with the supple human breathiness you might expect from a person who spends her days writing dialogue. It features lots of great punchlines. . . . It features occasional, chatty, second-person asides. . . . [It] is also in many ways a side-door self-help book . . . [with] pieces of advice that concern not just Rhimes's readers, but everyone. . . . *Year of Yes* is a book about the shifts taking place in Hollywood right now, and in the world right now, in the guise of a friendly memoir. It is, like Shondaland itself, making a statement. It is insisting that it is time for the people who used to be invisible to come forward and be seen."

—theatlantic.com

"It's important to read this book. All women should read this book. If you haven't read it yet, do. And if you have read it, give it to someone else to read. And now I'm going to go dance it out."

—huffingtonpost.com

"Small, charmingly odd, inspirational stories . . . Quite simply, it's a book about how she learned to take care of herself, and how you might be able to as well. Welcome your new life coach, Shonda Rhimes."

—*Vulture*

"Rhimes guides the reader through her transformative year long experiment, each chapter dealing with a different personal challenge for herself, and she lets us deep inside her brain, carefully laying out all of her fears and self-doubt. . . . candid and friendly, almost as if the two of you were catching up over drinks."

—slate.com

"Let *Scandal* creator Shonda Rhimes be your spirit guide with her new book."

—*Marie Claire*

"A self-help book dressed in casual clothes, lessons for living a better life told through relatable personal essays from the woman who set out to, in the course of a year, make her own better. . . . There's an uncanny familiarity to the journey Rhimes goes on. . . . Never do you feel preached at while reading Rhimes's book. This woman of huge fame and fortune is speaking directly to you, and she's doing it with familiarity, humor and earned wisdom. . . . *Year of Yes* is an awakening as much as it is a reckoning. Recognize the power of what you've been doing. Do more of it."

—thedailybeast.com

"A book that is fun, dishy and inspirational all at the same time . . . a powerful book, a great gift for a friend or yourself, whether you're a fan of the Shondaland lineup or not."

—Motherlode/nytimes.com

"You'll want to stand up and cheer when she takes control, remakes her life and learns to love herself."

—buzzfeed.com

"It's like having a mini–Shonda in your head, encouraging you to go for it. And say, 'It's handled.'"

—*The Skimm* (Skimm Reads pick)

"[The stories are] strung together with humor and vulnerability. . . . Rhimes speaks to the reader as though she's unloading to a longtime friend. . . . She excels at penning . . . depth and substance into *Year of Yes*. Ms. Rhimes avoids what could have been the book's biggest pitfall—being just another Hollywood read with a celeb lamenting the woes of fame."

—*Pittsburgh Post-Gazette*

"A State of the Rhimes speech punctuated by undeniably memorable turns of phrase . . . incredibly refreshing."

—*The Guardian* (US)

"This memoir/call to arms from the one-woman force behind *Grey's Anatomy*, *Scandal* and *How to Get Away with Murder* is basically a New Year's resolution between two covers. Wherever you're going, bring it with you."

—*Bloomberg Businessweek*

"Can help motivate even the most determined homebody to get out and try something new in the New Year."

—*Redeye*

"A sincere and inspiring account of saying yes to life . . . Rhimes tells us all about it in the speedy, smart style of her much-loved TV shows. She's warm, eminently relatable and funny. . . . The book is a fast read—readers could finish it in the time it takes to watch a full lineup of her Thursday night programing—but it's not insubstantial. Like a cashmere shawl you pack just in case, *Year of Yes* is well worth the purse space, and it would make an equally great gift. Rhimes said yes to sharing her insights. Following her may not land you on the cover of a magazine, but you'll be glad you did."

—*Kirkus Reviews*

"A powerful memoir and self-help book that promotes saying Yes! to life . . . [Rhimes] shares some of the key beliefs and events behind this transformation, all with good humor and vivid prose. Rhimes comes across as inspiring and real, every bit the heroine whom readers need to inspire such a change in themselves."

—publishersweekly.com

"A hilariously honest look at Rhimes's journey of overcoming her fears and saying yes. . . . Like Rhimes's television shows, *Year of Yes* is highly entertaining. . . . Rhimes's boundless, energetic prose pulls the reader through this fast-paced book, eager for more. In *Year of Yes*, like everything else she does, Rhimes makes success look easy. She inspires us to stop looking for ways to say no, and start looking for ways to overcome our own fears and say yes."

—*The Root*

"Rhimes's familiar, conversational writing style makes the book a more accessible *Lean In*, a self-help book and personal journal all rolled into one."

—tvguide.com

YEAR
of YES

SHONDA
RHIMES

**SIMON &
SCHUSTER**

London · New York · Sydney · Toronto · New Delhi

A CBS COMPANY

First published in Great Britain by Simon & Schuster UK Ltd, 2015
This paperback edition published by Simon & Schuster UK Ltd, 2016
A CBS COMPANY

7 9 10 8 6

Simon & Schuster UK Ltd
1st Floor
222 Gray's Inn Road
London WC1X 8HB

www.simonandschuster.co.uk
www.simonandschuster.com.au
www.simonandschuster.co.in

Simon & Schuster Australia, Sydney
Simon & Schuster India, New Delhi

The author and publishers have made all reasonable efforts
to contact copyright-holders for permission, and apologise
for any omissions or errors in the form of credits given.
Corrections may be made to future printings.

Some names and identifying characteristics have been changed,
and some individuals are portrayed as composites. The timeline of certain events
has been altered, with some events reordered, combined and/or compressed.
The author is neither truly old nor is she truly a liar.

Quotations from Grey's Anatomy and Private Practice courtesy of ABC Studios.

A CIP catalogue record for this book
is available from the British Library

Paperback ISBN: 978-1-4711-5732-5
eBook ISBN: 978-1-4711-5733-2

Interior design by Ruth Lee-Mui

Printed and bound by CPI Group (UK) Ltd, Croydon, CR0 4YY

Simon & Schuster UK Ltd are committed to sourcing paper
that is made from wood grown in sustainable forests and support the Forest
Stewardship Council, the leading international forest certification organisation.
Our books displaying the FSC logo are printed on FSC certified paper.

For Harper, Emerson and Beckett,

May every year be a Year of *Yes*. May you inherit a future that no longer requires you to be an F.O.D. And if it is the future and that hasn't happened yet, go ahead and start the revolution. Mommy says you can.

and

For Delorse,

For giving me permission to start my own private revolution. And for saying yes to showing up every single time I've called your name. You are the F.O.D. within the family—the five of us who came behind you thank you for creating our second chances.

The need for change bulldozed a road
down the center of my mind.

—MAYA ANGELOU

If you want crappy things to stop
happening to you, then stop accepting
crap and demand something more.

—CRISTINA YANG, *GREY'S ANATOMY*

Hello

I'm Old and I Like to Lie
(A Disclaimer of Sorts)

I'm a liar.

And I don't care who knows it.

I make stuff up all the time.

Before you start speculating about my character and my sanity . . . let me explain myself. I make stuff up because I have to. It's not just something I like to do. I mean, I *do* like to do it. I thoroughly enjoy making stuff up. Fingers-crossed-behind-my-back flights of fancy make my motor run, shake my groove thing, turn me on.

I *do* like to make stuff up.

I *love* it.

It's also kind of ingrained in me. My brain? My brain naturally just leans in the direction of half truths; my brain turns toward fiction. Like a flower to the sun. Like writing with my right hand. Fabrication is like a bad habit that feels good, easy to pick up, hard to quit. Spinning tall tales, knitting yarns made of stories, is my dirty little vice. And I like it.

But it's not *just* a bad habit. I need to do it. I have to do it.

It turns out that making stuff up?

Is a job.

For real.

Seriously.

The very thing that had me on my knees in church during recess reciting the rosary for one nun or another at St. Mary's Catholic School in Park Forest, Illinois, is an actual honest-to-Jesus-Mary-and-Joseph job.

"Don't tell anyone, but my Mom? She escaped from Russia. She was engaged to this guy, Vladimir—she had to leave the love of her life behind and everything. It's so sad. And now she has to pretend she's a totally regular American or we could all be killed. Of *course* I speak Russian. *Dah.* What? She's *black* Russian, stupid. Like white Russian. But black Russian. Anyway, it doesn't matter what kind of Russian, we can never go there ever, she's a dead woman over there now. For trying to assassinate Leonid Brezhnev. What do you mean *why*? Don't you know anything? To stop nuclear winter. To save America. Duh."

You'd think I'd get extra credit for knowing who Leonid Brezhnev was. You'd think I'd get bonus points for reading up on Russian politics. You'd think someone would thank me for educating my fellow ten-year-olds about the Cold War.

Knees. Church. Nuns. Rosary.

I can recite the rosary in my sleep. I *have* recited the rosary in my sleep.

Making stuff up is responsible for that. Making stuff up is responsible for everything—everything I've done, everything I am, everything I have. Without the tales, the fiction, the stories I've spun, it is highly likely that right now, today, I'd be a very quiet librarian in Ohio.

Instead, the figments of my imagination altered whatever downward path the nuns at school expected my life to take.

The stuff I made up carried me from the small bedroom I shared with my sister Sandie in the suburbs of Chicago to an Ivy League dorm room in the hills of New Hampshire, and then it took me all the way to Hollywood.

My destiny rides squarely on the back of my imagination.

The sinful stories that earned me prayer as penance during recess are the same stories that now allow me to buy a bottle of wine plus a steak at the grocery store and not worry about the price. Being able to buy wine and steak and not think about the price is very important to me. It was a goal. Because when I was a struggling graduate student in film school, I often had no money. And so I often had to *choose* between wine and things like toilet paper. Steak did not even enter into the equation.

It was wine or toilet paper.

Wine.

Or.

Toilet paper.

The toilet paper did not always win.

Did I just see you give me a look? Was that . . . did you just *judge* me?

No. You are *not* about to come up into this book and judge me.

That is *not* how we are going to start off this journey. We are gonna ease on down the road. We're in this book together, my friend. So let she who is without wine cast the first stone. Otherwise . . .

Sometimes the toilet paper does not win.

Sometimes a broke woman needs the red wine more.

So you'll have to cut me some slack if I'm unapologetic about my love for the magic of a little bit of fibbing and invention.

Because I make stuff up for a living.

Imagining is now my job. I write television shows. I make up characters. I create whole worlds in my head. I add words to the lexicon of daily conversation—maybe you talk about your *vajayjay* and tell your friend that someone at work got *Poped* because of my shows. I birth babies, I end lives. I dance it out. I wear the white hat. I operate. I gladiate. I exonerate. I spin yarns and tell tall tales and sit around the campfire. I wrap myself in fiction. Fiction is my job. Fiction is it. Fiction is everything. Fiction is my *jam*.

Yes, I'm a liar.

But now I'm a *professional* liar.

Grey's Anatomy was my first real job in television. Having a show I created be my first real TV job meant that I knew nothing about working in TV when I began running my own show. I asked every TV writer I bumped into what this job was like, what being in charge of a season of a network television drama was like. I got loads of great advice, most of which made clear that every show was a very different, specific experience. With one exception: every single writer I met likened writing for television to one thing—laying track for an oncoming speeding train.

The story is the track and you gotta keep laying it down because of the train. That train is production. You keep writing, you keep laying track down, no matter what, because the train of production is coming toward you—no matter what. Every eight days, the crew needs to begin to prepare a new episode—find locations, build sets, design costumes, find props, plan shots. And every eight days after that, the crew needs to *film* a new episode. Every eight days. Eight days to prep. Eight days to shoot. Eight days, eight days, eight days, eight days. Which means every eight days, that crew needs a brand-new script. And my job is to damn well provide them with one. Every. Eight. Days. That train of production is a'coming. Every eight days that crew on that soundstage better have something to shoot. Because the worst thing you can do is halt or derail production and cost the studio hundreds of thousands of dollars while everyone waits. That is how you go from being a TV writer to being a failed TV writer.

So I learned to lay track quickly. Artfully. Creatively. But as fast as freaking lightning.

Lay some fiction on it.

Smooth some story into that gap.

Nail some imagination around those edges.

I always feel the heat of the speeding train on the backs of my thighs, on the heels of my feet, on my shoulder blades and elbows, on the seat of my pants as it threatens to run me down. But I don't step back and let the cool wind hit my face as I watch the train speed by. I never step back. Not because I can't. Because I don't want to. That is not the gig. And for me, there is no better gig on the face of the earth. The adrenaline, the rush, the ... I call it the *hum*. There's a hum that happens inside my head when I hit a certain writing rhythm, a certain speed. When laying track goes from feeling like climbing a mountain on my hands and knees to feeling like flying effortlessly through the air. Like breaking the sound barrier. Everything inside me just shifts. I break the writing barrier. And the feeling of laying track changes, transforms, shifts from exertion into exultation.

I've gotten good at it, the making stuff up.

I could lie in the Olympics.

But there's another problem.

I am old.

Not shake-my-fist-and-holler-if-you-run-across-my-lawn old. And not revered-wrinkled-elder old. I'm not old on the outside. I mean, on the outside, I look *good*.

I look *young*.

I don't look old and probably never will. Seriously. I will never age. Not because I am a vampire or anything.

I will never age because I am my mother's child.

My mother? Looks incredible. At most, on a bad day, she looks like a slightly worried twenty-five-year-old who maybe partied a little too hard last night. I mean, the woman is nearing . . . she won't like it if I tell you. So let's just put it this way. my mother has six children, seventeen grandchildren and eight great-grandchildren. When I see her, I like to tell her that she is "keeping it tight." Mainly because it appalls her. Also because it makes her laugh. Mostly because we all know it's true. But secretly I say it because it's something of a relief to me—I know I've got that face to look forward to.

The women in my family? We've won the genetic lottery.

You think I'm kidding?

I'm not kidding.

When I get older, I will stand in line along with the rest of the women on my mother's side of the family and enjoy the benefits that come with cashing in that winning ticket. Because we didn't just win that lottery, we won the Powerball, baby. All six numbers—even the big red one.

My aunts, my cousins, my sisters . . . you should see us all standing around looking like toddlers in tiaras. We women, we descendants of my grandmother Rosie Lee? We look damn good. Our black don't crack—*for real*. As my sister Sandie and I like to remind each other, "We will always be the hottest women in the old folks' home."

And that is the thing that is so bittersweet and sad. Because my brain.

My brain. Oh, my brain.

My brain, she is old.

Really old.

Gumming-her-food old.

So, yes. Yes, I will be one of the two hottest women residing at the Sunset Senior Citizens Center for Old Folks Who Don't Want to Live Like *Grey Gardens*.

But while I most certainly will be a belle of that senior ball, I will not remember that I ever thought being hot in an old folks' home was a fun thing to be.

I may have won the genetic lottery on the outside, but on the inside . . .

We are choosing between wine and toilet paper up in here, okay?

My memory sucks.

It's subtle. Perhaps if I didn't spend my entire day needing to express myself, needing to pull words out of my head, I'd have never noticed it. But I do. So I did. Maybe if my first TV show hadn't been a medical show that sent me screaming to a doctor with hypochondriacal certainties of tumors and diseases every time I sneezed, I would shrug it off as lack of sleep. But it was. So I can't.

Names are forgotten, details of one event are switched with another, a crazy story I am sure was told by one friend was actually told by someone else. The insides of my brain are a fading photograph, stories and images drifting away to places unknown. Leaving patches of nothingness where a name or an event or a location should be.

Anyone who has watched *Grey's Anatomy* knows that I am obsessed with curing Alzheimer's. Anyone who knows me even vaguely knows that my greatest fear is getting Alzheimer's.

So I'm absolutely sure I have it. I'm *sure* I have Alzheimer's. So sure that I take my crappy memory and my shrieking hypochondria to the doctor.

I don't have Alzheimer's.

Yet.

(Thank you, universe. You are pretty and smart. So pretty and so smart.)

I don't have Alzheimer's.

I'm just old.

Pour one out for my youth.

Time is simply not my friend. My memory is ever-so-slowly being replaced by blank spaces. The details of my life are disappearing. The paintings are being stolen off the walls of my brain.

It's exhausting. And confusing. And sometimes funny. And often sad.

But.

I make stuff up for a living. Been doing it all my life. So.

Without ever committing to a plan, without ever actively trying, without even realizing it is going to happen, the story-teller inside me steps forward and solves the problem. My inner liar leaps in to take over my brain and begins to spin the yarns. Begins to just . . . fill in the blank spaces. To paint over the nothingness. To close the gaps and connect the dots.

To lay track for the train.

The train that is a'coming no matter what.

Because that's the gig, baby.

Putting fiction on it is where it is *at*.

Which leaves me with a conundrum.

This book is not fiction. It's not about characters that I made up. It doesn't take place at Seattle Grace or Pope & Associates. It's about me. It takes place in reality. It's supposed to be *just* the facts.

Which means I can't embellish. I can't add a little here or there. I can't put a bit of sparkly ribbon or a handful of glitter on it. I can't create a better ending or insert a more exciting twist. I can't just say screw it and go for the good story and say a rosary later.

I can't make stuff up. I need to tell you the truth. All I have to work with is the truth. But it's *my* truth. And therein lies the problem.

You get that, right?

So. This is my disclaimer, I suppose.

Is every single solitary word of this book true?

I hope so.

I think so.

I believe so.

But how in the hell would I remember if it wasn't?

I'm old.

I like to make stuff up.

Okay. It's possible. There could be some track in here. I could have laid track for the train all up in these pages. I didn't mean to. I didn't try to. I don't think I did. But it's possible.

I'll say this. This is the truth I remember. The truth as I know it. As much as an old liar can know. I'm doing my best. And so if I didn't get every detail correct, well . . .

. . . once more for the cheap seats, everybody . . .

I'm old.

And I like to lie.

Prologue

Full Frontal

When it was first suggested to me that I write about this year, my first instinct was to say no.

Writing about myself feels a lot like I have just decided to stand up on a table in a very proper restaurant, raise my dress and show everyone that I'm not wearing panties.

That is to say, it feels *shocking*.

It puts the bits of me that I usually keep to myself on display.

Naughty bits.

Secret bits.

See, I am an introvert. Deep. To the bone. My marrow is introvert marrow. My snot is introvert snot. Every cell in my body screams continuously at me with every word I type that writing this book is an unnatural act.

A lady never shows her soul outside the boudoir.

Showing you a bit of full-frontal *me* makes me nervous and twitchy, like I have a rash in an unfortunate place. It makes me breathe really hard in a weird panicked dog–sounding way. It makes me laugh inappropriately in public spaces whenever I think about people reading it.

Writing this book makes me uncomfortable.

And that, dear reader, is the point. It's the whole thing. Which is why I am writing it anyway. Despite the twitching and the laughing and the breathing.

Being too comfortable is what started all of this in the first place.

Well, being too comfortable plus hearing six startling words.

Plus turkey.

YEAR
of YES

1

NO

"You never say yes to anything."

Six startling words.

That's the beginning. That's the origin of it all. My sister Delorse said six startling words and changed everything. She said six words and now, as I write this, I have become a different person.

"You never say yes to anything."

She didn't even *say* the six startling words. She muttered them, really. Her lips barely moving, her eyes fixed intently on the large knife in her hands as she was dicing vegetables at a furious pace, trying to beat the clock.

*yes*yes*yes*yes*yes*yes*yes*yes*yes*yes*yes*yes*yes*yes*yes*yes

It's November 28, 2013.

Thanksgiving Day morning. So obviously, the stakes are high.

Thanksgiving and Christmas have always been my mother's domain. She has ruled our family holidays with flawless perfection. Food always delicious, flowers always fresh, colors coordinated. Everything perfect.

Last year, my mother announced that she was tired of doing all the work. Yes, she made it *look* effortless—that did not mean it *was* effortless. So, still reigning supreme, my mother declared she was abdicating her throne.

Now, this morning, is Delorse's first time stepping up to wear the crown.

This has made my sister intense and dangerous.

She doesn't even bother glancing up at me when she mutters the words. There is no time. Hungry family and friends will bear down on us in less than three hours. We have not even reached the turkey-basting segment of the cooking process. So unless my sister can kill me, cook me and serve me with stuffing, gravy and cranberry sauce, I am not getting her full attention right now.

"You never say yes to anything."

Delorse is the eldest child in our family. I am the youngest. Twelve years separate us; that age gap is filled by our brothers and sisters—Elnora, James, Tony and Sandie. With so many siblings between us, growing up, it was easy to feel as though the two of us existed in the same solar system but never visited each other's planets. After all, Delorse was heading off to college as I was entering kindergarten. I have vague childhood memories of her—Delorse cornrowing my hair way too tightly, giving me a braid headache; Delorse teaching my older brothers and sisters how to do a brand-new dance called The Bump; Delorse walking down the aisle at her wedding, my sister Sandie and me behind her holding up the train of her gown, our father at her side. As a child, she was the role model of the kind of woman I was supposed to grow up to be. As an adult, she's one of my best friends. Most of the important memories of my grown-up life include her. So I suppose it is fitting that she is here now, muttering these words at me. It is fitting that right now she's the one both telling me who I am supposed to grow up to be *and* standing at the center of what will become one of the most important memories of my life.

And this moment *is* important.

She doesn't know it. I don't know it. Not right now. Right now this moment doesn't feel important at all. Right now, this feels like Thanksgiving morning and she's tired.

She got up before dawn to call and remind me to take the twenty-one-pound turkey out of the refrigerator to settle. Then she drove the four blocks from her house to mine in order to do all the cooking for our big family dinner. It's not quite eleven a.m. but she's already been at it for hours. Chopping, stirring, seasoning. She's working really hard.

And I have been watching her.

It's not as bad as it sounds.

I'm not doing *nothing*.

I'm not *useless*.

I've been handing her things when she asks. Also, I have my three-month-old daughter strapped to my chest in a baby sling and my one-and-a-half-year-old daughter on my hip. I've combed my eleven-year-old's hair, turned off the TV show she was watching and forced a book into the child's hands.

And we're talking. My sister and I. We're talking. Catching up on all the things we have missed since, well . . . yesterday or maybe the day before.

Okay. Fine. *I'm* talking.

I'm talking. She's cooking. I'm talking and talking and *talking*. I have a lot to tell her. I'm listing for her all of the invitations that I've received in the last week or so. Someone wants me to speak at this conference and someone invited me to go to that fancy party and I've been asked to travel to such-and-such country to meet that king or to be on a certain talk show. I list ten or eleven invitations I received. I tell her about all of them in detail.

I will admit to you right now that I toss in a few extra juicy bits, spin a few tales, lay some track. I'm purposely boasting a little bit—I am trying to get a reaction out of my big sister. I want her to be impressed. I want her to think I'm cool.

Look, I was raised in a great family. My parents and siblings have many wonderful qualities. They are universally pretty and smart. And like I said, they all look like fetuses. But the members of my immediate family all share one hugely disgusting criminal flaw.

They do not give a crap about my job.

At all.

None of 'em.

Not a one.

They are frankly disturbed that anyone would be impressed by me. For any reason. People behaving toward me as though I might be vaguely interesting bewilders them deeply. They stare at one another, baffled, whenever someone treats me as anything other than what they know me to be—their deeply dorky, overly verbal, baby sister.

Hollywood is a bizarre place. It's easy to lose touch with reality here. But nothing keeps a person grounded like a host of siblings who, when someone requests your autograph, ask in a truly horrified tone, "Her? Shonda's autograph? Are you sure? Shonda? No wait, really, *Shonda*? Shonda *RHIMES*? *Why?*"

It's super rude. And yet . . . think of how many bloated egos would be saved if everyone had five older brothers and sisters. They love me. A lot. But they are not gonna stand for any celebrity VIP crap from the kid in Coke-bottle glasses they all saw throw up alphabet soup all over the back porch and then slip face-first in the vomit chunks.

Which is why right now I'm verbally tap-dancing around

the room, shaking it like I'm competing for a mirror-ball trophy. I'm trying to get my sister to show any sign of being impressed, a glimmer that she might think I'm remotely cool. Trying to get a reaction from these people I'm related to, well, it has almost become a game for me. A game I believe that one day I *will* win.

But not today. My sister doesn't even bother to blink in my direction. Instead, impatient, possibly tired and likely sick of the sound of my voice going on and on about my list of fancy invitations, she cuts me off.

"Are you going to do any of these things?"

I pause. A little taken aback.

"Huh?" That's what I say. "Huh?"

"These events. These parties, conferences, talk shows. Did you say yes to any of them?"

I stand there for a moment. Silent. Confused.

What is she talking about? Say yes?

"Well. No, I mean . . . no," I stammer, "I can't say . . . obviously I said no. I mean, I'm busy."

Delorse keeps her head down. Keeps chopping.

Later, when I think about it, I will realize she was probably not even listening to me. She was probably thinking about whether or not she had enough cheddar grated for the mac and cheese she had to make next. Or deciding how many pies to bake. Or wondering how she was going to get out of cooking Thanksgiving dinner next year. But in the moment, I don't get that. In the moment, my sister keeping her head down? It MEANS something. In the moment, my sister keeping her head down feels purposeful.

Deep.

Challenging.

Rude.

I have to defend myself. How do I defend myself? What do I—

At that exact moment (and this is so fortuitous I decide the universe *loves* me), Beckett, the sunny three-month-old baby strapped to my chest, decides to spit up a geyser of milk that runs down the front of my shirt in a creepy warm waterfall. On my hip, my prudish one-and-a-half-year-old, the moon to Beckett's sun, wrinkles her nose.

"I smell something, honey," she tells me. Emerson calls everyone "honey." As I nod at her and dab at the smelly hot milk stain, I pause. Take in the mess in my arms.

And I have my defense.

"Beckett! Emerson! I have babies!! *And* Harper! I have a tween! Tweens are delicate flowers! I can't just go places and do things!!! I have children to take care of!"

I holler this across the counter in my sister's general direction.

Wait. Speaking of taking care of stuff . . . I also have to take care of a little something called Thursday nights. Ha! I do a victory shimmy across the kitchen and point at her. Gloating.

"I also have a job! Two jobs! *Grey's Anatomy* AND *Scandal*! Three children and two jobs! I'm . . . busy! I am a mother! I'm a writer! I run shows!"

Bam!

I feel totally triumphant. I'm a mother. A *mother*, damn it. I have children. THREE children. And I'm running two television shows at one time. I have more than six hundred crew members depending on me for work. I'm a mother who works. I'm a working mother.

Like . . . Beyoncé.

Yes.

Exactly like Beyoncé.

I am bringing home the bacon AND frying it up in the pan. It's not an excuse. It's a fact. No one can argue with that. No one can argue with Beyoncé.

But I forgot that this is Delorse.

Delorse can argue with anyone.

Delorse puts down her knife. She actually stops cooking and puts down her knife. Then she raises her head to look up at me. My sister, the biggest winner in our family's genetic Powerball, is in her fifties. Late fifties. Her sons are grown men with degrees and careers. She has grandchildren. And yet I am often asked if my fifty-seven-year-old sister *is my child*.

The horror of it is sometimes too much.

So when she raises her head to look at me, she looks more

like a saucy fourteen-year-old than she does my eldest sibling. Her saucy-fourteen-year-old face eyes me.

"Shonda."

That's all she says. But it's said with such confidence . . .

So I blurt out—

"A *single* mother."

Now, that is shameless. You and I both know it. Because while the technical definition of "single mother" fits me—I am a mother, I am single—its cultural and colloquial meaning does not. Trying to appropriate that term as if I am a struggling mom doing my best to put food on the table makes me an ass. I know it. You know it. And unfortunately? Delorse also knows it.

I need to put an end to the conversation. I raise an eyebrow and make my bossy face. The one I make at the office when I need everyone to stop arguing with me.

My sister does not give a crap about my bossy face. But she picks up her knife again, goes back to chopping.

"Wash the celery," she tells me.

So I wash celery. Somehow the smell of fresh celery, the motion of the washing, Emerson's joy as she splashes the water over the counter, it all lulls me into a false sense of security.

Which is why I am not prepared.

I turn. Hand her the wet, clean celery. And I'm surprised when, still chopping, Delorse begins to speak.

"You are a single mother but you are not a *single mother*. I live four blocks away. Sandie lives four blocks away. Your parents live forty minutes away and would love to stay with the kids. You have literally the best nanny in the world. You have three amazing best friends who would step in and help at any time. You are surrounded by family and friends who love you, people who want you to be happy. You are your own boss—your job is only as busy as you make it. But you never do anything but work. You never have any fun. You used to have *so much fun*. Now, all of these amazing opportunities are coming your way—once-in-a-lifetime opportunities—and you aren't taking advantage of any of them. Why?"

I shift, uncomfortable. For some reason, I do not like this. I don't like anything about this conversation at all. My life is fine. My life is great. I mean, look around!

Look!

I'm . . . happy.

Ish.

I'm happyish.

Kind of.

Mind your own business, Delorse. You are annoying, Delorse. People aren't supposed to Benjamin Button so your face is clearly the result of a pact with Satan, Delorse! You know what, Delorse? You smell like poop.

But I don't say any of that. Instead I stand there for a long time. Watching her chop. And finally, I answer. Putting just the right amount of casual arrogance in my voice.

"Whatever."

And then I turn away, hoping to indicate that the conversation is over. I head over to the sitting area, where I gently settle an already napping Beckett into the bassinet. I place Emerson on the changing table for a fresh diaper. In a moment, I'll go upstairs and try to find a spit-up-free shirt to wear for dinner. The fresh diaper is on. I put Emerson on my hip, lay her head on my shoulder, and we swing back around to face my sister as I head for the stairs. That's when she says it. The six words.

Mutters them. Almost under her breath.

As she finishes chopping the onions.

Six startling words.

"You never say yes to anything."

For a single beat, time stops. Becomes a clear, frozen moment I'll never forget. One of the paintings that will never be taken from my mental wall. My sister, in a brown hoodie, her hair in a neat knot at the nape of her neck, standing there with that knife in her hand, head down, the little pile of white onion pieces on the cutting board before her.

She tosses the words out there.

"You never say yes to anything."

Tosses the words out there like a grenade.

You never say yes to anything.

Then my sister slides the onions over and begins chopping the celery. I head upstairs to change my shirt. Family and friends arrive. The turkey cooks perfectly. Dinner is delicious.

The grenade lies there in the middle of everything. Quiet. Camouflaged. I don't think about it.

You never say yes to anything.

Thanksgiving Day comes and goes.

2

Maybe?

The grenade sits dormant for several weeks.

It rolls around in my brain, the safety clip firmly in place. So quietly stealthy that I am able to forget it is there. I maintain my usual routine. I go to work, I write scripts, I work on episodes of TV, I come home, I snuggle babies, I read bedtime stories.

Life is normal.

One single out-of-the-ordinary event occurs: I fly to Washington as a new trustee of the Kennedy Center. I attend the celebrations, making my first trip to the White House. And then, for magical reasons that to this day I still don't understand, I am told I will be sitting with the president and the First Lady in their box at the Kennedy Center Honors.

I am not asked. I am told. I am not given a chance to say

no. Mainly because I am sure it never occurs to anyone that I would decline such an honor. Who would?

I wear a very beautiful black beaded evening gown. My date wears a new tuxedo. We sit right behind President and Mrs. Obama for the entirety of the ceremony. I am much too shy and nervous to croak out more than a few words when faced with a chance to speak to the actual president and First Lady. I certainly don't form sentences. But I enjoy myself. I have fun.

We drink cocktails in the same room as Carlos Santana and Shirley MacLaine. We get the street cred to be able to say we were there when Snoop Dogg thanked Herbie Hancock for creating hip-hop. We see Garth Brooks sing Billy Joel's "Goodnight Saigon" with a choir made up of veterans. It's amazing. The whole evening feels a bit enchanted. No matter how cynical the Beltway thinks it is or how world-weary politicians may seem, D.C. is a town that lacks the true cynicism of Hollywood. People actually get excited about things there and the enthusiasm is infectious. I fly back to Los Angeles filled with a buoyant sense of optimism.

The grenade explodes without warning.

It happens at four in the morning a few days before Christmas. I'm flat on my back in the middle of my king-size bed. Eyes pulled open against my will. Something's snapped me awake, yanked me out of sleep.

Being woken abruptly is not new.

Like every other mother on the planet, from the moment my first baby entered the house, I stopped getting real sleep. Motherhood means I'm always a little bit awake, a little bit alert at all times. One eye open. So being awakened by something in the middle of the night isn't surprising. What is surprising is that this something doesn't have anything to do with a furious kid standing in a crib screaming her head off. The house is silent. My girls are fast asleep.

So why am I awake?

If they had asked me, I would have said no.

That thought makes me sit up in bed.

What?

If they had asked me, I would have said no.

My face gets hot. I'm embarrassed, as if there is someone else in the room hearing the words inside my brain.

If they had asked me if I wanted to sit in the presidential box at the Kennedy Center Honors, I would have said no.

Ridiculous.

But it's true. It's clearly true.

I am as sure of this as I am of the need to breathe. I would have said no carefully. Respectfully. Graciously. I would have come up with a creative excuse, expressed both extreme honor and regret. The excuse would have been good, the excuse would have been *brilliant*.

I mean, come on.

I'm a writer. I would have been eloquent and delightful—

no one can decline an invitation as beautifully as I can. You're all amateurs at bailing on something; I bail on events so well that I can do it in the major leagues.

I nod to myself. Certain. However I handled it, I definitely would have said no. That is an unquestionable fact.

If they had asked, I would have said no.

Seriously?

I am up and out of bed. Sleep doesn't have a chance now. This requires thought. This requires wine. Downstairs, I throw myself on my sofa and stare at the lights of my Christmas tree. Glass of wine in hand, I drink about the question.

Why would I have said no?

But I know the answer. I knew the answer before I got out of bed. I just wanted the wine.

Because it's scary.

I would have said no to sitting in the presidential box at the Kennedy Center with POTUS and FLOTUS because the prospect of saying yes was terrifying to me.

I would have said no because if I had said yes, I would have had to actually *do* it. I would have had to actually go and sit in the box and be there to meet the president and the First Lady. I would have had to make small talk and say things. I would have had to drink cocktails near Carlos Santana.

I would have had to do all of the things that I, in fact, *did do* that night.

And I had a wonderful time. When all was said and done, it was one of the most memorable nights of my life.

Look, I am known for giving good story.

The kind of good story told over dinner that makes my friends laugh, that gets my date to accidentally spit his cocktail across a table. The kind of good story that has everyone asking me to "tell that one again." That's my superpower—telling good stories. Smooth stories. Funny stories. Epic stories.

I can make any story good. I can take the lamest tale and make it compelling. The thing is, a good story is not about purposely lying. The best stories are true. Giving good story just requires that I . . . leave out the untidy bits.

The bits where, before I leave for the White House, I spend ten minutes convincing myself that I do not have the stomach flu, that I am fine. Where I consider licking the dust at the bottom of the Xanax bottle because oh yeah, I don't *take* Xanax anymore, it's been twelve years since Xanax was my friend. *Yuck, this Xanax dust is twelve-year-old Xanax dust?*

Where I sleep for fourteen hours straight because I am so numb with stress that it's either sleep or run. And I don't mean jog on a treadmill. I mean, run. I mean, get in a car, go to the airport, get on a plane and run away.

Run.

That seems like a much better plan than going out in public with every nerve ending in my body screaming.

This is who I am.

Silent.

Quiet.

Interior.

More comfortable with books than new situations.

Content to live within my imagination.

I've lived inside my head since I was a kid. My earliest memories are of sitting on the floor of the kitchen pantry. I stayed there for hours in the darkness and warmth, playing with a kingdom I created out of the canned goods.

I was not an unhappy kid. Because I was the baby in a family of eight, at any given moment, someone was available to read to me, applaud whatever story I had come up with or let me listen in on their teenage secrets. The end to every sibling argument over the extra cookie or the last slice of cake was always an egalitarian sigh: "Give it to the baby."

I was loved, I was a star, I was the Blue Ivy of my world. I was not an unhappy kid.

I was just an unusual kid.

Lucky for me, my parents held the unusual in high regard. And so when I wanted to play with the cans in the pantry for hours on end, my mother didn't tell me to stop messing around with the food and go somewhere else to play. Instead, she declared it a sign of creativity, closed the pantry door and let me be.

You have her to thank for my love of long-form serialized drama.

The world I created inside the small closet filled with canned goods and cereal was serious; these days I would describe it as a winter-is-coming-where-are-my-dragons kind of solo play date, but this was not HBO. This was the suburbs in the 1970s. We didn't need reality TV because TV was *real*. Nixon was going down. As Watergate played out on the tiny black and white set my mother had dragged into the kitchen and balanced on a chair just outside the pantry doors, my three-year-old imagination made a world of its own. The big cans of yams ruled over the peas and green beans while the tiny citizens of Tomato Paste Land planned a revolution designed to overthrow the government. There were hearings and failed assassination attempts and resignations. Every once in a while, my mom would open the pantry door, flooding my world with light. She'd politely tell me she needed vegetables for dinner. The canned judiciary would sentence a can of corn to death for treason and I'd deliver the guilty party into the hands of the executioner.

Man, that pantry was fun.

You see the problem? Did you *read* the problem?

Man, that pantry was fun.

That just came out of my mouth. I actually said it aloud WHILE I typed it. And I said it without any irony. I said it with a big dorky wistful grin on my face.

I had a wonderful childhood, but I lived so deep in my imagination that I was happier and more at home in that pantry with the canned goods than I ever was with people. I felt safer in the pantry. Freer in that pantry. True when I was three years old.

And somehow even *more* true at forty-three.

As I sit on my sofa staring into the Christmas lights, I realize that I would still be partying in my pantry if I thought I could get away with it. If I didn't have children who needed me to be in the world. I fight the instinct every day. Which is why I now have a garden for vegetables.

If they had asked, I would have said no.

I would have said no.

Because I always say no.

And that's when the grenade explodes.

Suddenly it's Thanksgiving and I'm back in that kitchen, covered in spit-up, watching my sister chop those onions. And I understand her now.

You never say yes to anything.

I don't just understand her—*I believe her.* I hear her. And I know. She is right.

BOOM.

Grenade.

When the dust settles and everything is clear, I am left with one thought rattling through my head.

I'm miserable.

That makes me put down my wineglass. Am I drunk? Am I *kidding* me? Did I just think that?

Honestly, I'm a little indignant with myself. I'm embarrassed to even be having that thought. I'm ashamed, if you really wanna know. I'm bathed in shame.

I'm miserable?

I'm still a little ashamed to be telling you that right now.

I'm miserable.

Who in the hell do I think I am?

A whiner. That's who. A great big old whiner person.

You know who gets to be miserable? Malala. Because *someone shot her in the face.* You know who else? The Chibok schoolgirls. Because the terrorist group Boko Haram kidnapped them from school for forced marriage (which is just like regular marriage except exactly the opposite and full of rape) and *no one cares anymore.* You know who else? Anne Frank. Because she and about six million other Jewish people were murdered by Nazis. And? Mother Teresa. Because everyone else was too lazy to treat the lepers and so she had to do it.

It's pretty shameful of me to sit around saying I'm miserable when there are no bullets in my face and no one's kidnapped me or killed me or left me alone to treat all the lepers.

I grew up in a family where hard work was not optional. My parents worked very hard to raise and educate six—count 'em, *six*—children. And at some point, it dawned on me that the reason I had such a great childhood and never wanted for anything was because my parents worked extremely hard so we could have crazy things like food and gas and clothes and tuition. In high school, I got a job scooping ice cream at Baskin-Robbins and I have had a job ever since. So I am very aware that these days I live in a rarefied world. I know that I am extremely fortunate. I know that I have incredible children, a fantastic family, great friends, a spectacular job, a lovely home and all my arms, legs, fingers, toes and organs intact. I know I don't have the right to complain. Not about my life in comparison to anyone else's life. Unless that anyone is Beyoncé.

Damn, my life is so bad next to Beyoncé's life. So is yours. *Everyone's* life is so bad next to hers. If you know otherwise, if you know that Beyoncé's life is terrible for some reason, please, do not come up to me on the street and correct me. I need to believe that Beyoncé's life is perfect. It keeps me going.

But except for Beyoncé, I know how fortunate I am. I have no delusions that I am suffering in any real, true way. And so it *does* embarrass me to say it. I mean, you don't hear Malala complaining.

But you know why you don't hear Malala complaining?

Because Malala and her spiritual buddies Mother Teresa and Anne Frank are all MUCH better people than I am. Obviously. Because I'm clearly a giant whining baby and I suck. Because in that predawn, staring at my Christmas lights, even though I am ashamed, I cannot avoid it. The realization feels like plunging into an icy lake:

I am miserable.

Admitting this takes my breath away. I feel as though I am revealing new information to myself. Learning a secret I've been keeping from myself.

I am miserable.

Truly, deeply unhappy.

In December 2013, I was incredibly successful. I had two hugely popular television shows on the air—*Grey's Anatomy* and *Scandal*—and had just retired a third, *Private Practice*. My company, Shondaland, was in the midst of working with writer Peter Nowalk to develop a show that would soon become our newest hit, *How to Get Away with Murder*. So yeah, from the outside, I think everything probably looked great. And as long as I was writing, as long as my fingers were on the keyboard, as long as I was at Seattle Grace or Pope & Associates, as long as I was laying track and feeling the *hum* in my brain . . . I was fine. I was happy.

I know that I certainly tried to project the idea that my life was perfect. And I tried not to think about it too hard.

I went to work. I worked a lot. I came home. I spent time with my kids. I spent time with the guy I was dating. I slept. That's it.

In public, I smiled. A lot. I did a HUGE amount of smiling. And I did what I called "Athlete Talk." Athlete Talk is what happens on all of those interviews that take place right after any pro sports event you see on TV. A boxing match or an NBA game. Serena Williams smashing some record in tennis. Olympic swimming.

Good Athlete Talk is when the athlete goes before the press and keeps a smile on her face, voice bland and pleasant as she deftly fields one reporter's question after the other—never once saying anything of controversy or substance. My favorite Athlete Talker of all time is Michael Jordan. He'd stand there after scoring 5,635 points in one game, sweat pouring down his head, towering over some tiny reporter:

"I'm just happy to be playing the game of basketball," he'd say, smiling.

But, Michael, how do you feel about famine, politics, the WNBA, cartoons, Hanes underwear, tacos, anything?

"I'm thrilled to do what I can for the ball club. The Bulls are home to me," he'd chuckle pleasantly. And then he'd amble away. Presumably to the locker room, where he stopped being a Good Athlete Talker and started being a PERSON.

I was a Good Athlete Talker that year.

"I am just happy to be working for ABC."

"It's not my job to question my time slot. My job is to make the shows."

"I'm proud to be a part of the ABC team."

"I'm thrilled to do what I can for the network. ABC is home to me."

"I'm just happy to be playing the game of basketba—I mean, writing for TV."

And it was true. I was happy and proud and thrilled. I did like ABC. (I still do. Hello, ABC!) Just as I'm sure Michael truly liked the Bulls. But that Athlete Talk didn't have anything to do with liking my job.

It had to do with staying inside the pantry.

Keeping that door shut. Hearing Nixon on the outside. Only reaching one arm out into the sliver of light to hand out peas or corn or yams. Giving the people what they wanted. Then closing that door again.

Any actual parts of me, anything real, anything human, anything honest, I kept to myself. I was a very good girl. I did what everyone needed me to do.

And at the end of every day, as a reward, I poured myself a glass of red wine.

Red wine was joy in Shondaland.

yesyesyesyesyesyesyesyesyesyesyesyesyesyesyesyes

I used to be a really happy person. A *vibrant* person. I may have been shy and introverted but I had a rowdy, fun crowd of friends, some of whom I'd known since college and, with them around me, I was dance-on-the-tables Shonda, drive-to-New-Orleans-at-a-moment's-notice Shonda, adventurous-and-always-up-for-anything Shonda. Where did she go?

I had no real way to account for my unhappiness. For once, the storyteller had nothing to tell. I had no idea *why* I was unhappy, no specific moment or reason to point to. I just knew it was true.

Whatever that spark is that makes each one of us alive and unique . . . mine had gone. Stolen like the paintings on the wall. The flickering flame responsible for lighting me up from the inside, making me glow, keeping me warm . . . my candle had been blown out. I was shut down. I was tired. I was afraid. Small. Quiet.

The lives of my characters had become unimaginably huge. People all over the world knew Meredith and Olivia. At the same time, my life had so drained of color and excitement that I could barely see it.

Why?

You never say yes to anything.

Oh yeah. That.

I put down the glass of wine and lay on the sofa. And really thought about those six words.

You never say yes to anything.

Maybe it was time to start saying yes.

Maybe.

3

Umm, Yes . . . ?

January 13 is my birthday.

Yippee.

I love birthdays.

Because I love birthday parties.

When I found out there was something called a Puppy Party? Where they bring PUPPIES for kids to hold and cuddle for an hour and it's not puppy abuse, it's good for the puppies because they are training the puppies to be service dogs? I almost lost my mind jumping up and down. Puppies! A party with puppies! COME ON! That exists?

I like puppy parties and face painters and candy buffets and that guy with a guitar singing silly songs and ice cream and even some (very few, non-scary) clowns. And if you are past the age where helium balloons and face painting get you so excited and/or terrified that there's a danger you will pee your pants, I like dance parties and costume parties and dinner parties and seventies disco parties. I'm a firm believer that parties make everything better.

You'd think a shy person would hate birthday parties. I love them. Small parties and big parties. I don't necessarily love to *attend* them but I love the magic of them. I love the *idea* of them. I love to hug the corners of the walls and watch the good times. I love being with friends.

But today? This birthday?

I get out of the shower and lean really close to the bathroom mirror. So close I can see all my pores. Then I glare at my face.

"So you made it out of a uterus a long time ago. Big deal," I whisper. "So did *everybody else* on the planet. What else you got?"

Then I think about going back to bed.

Really. I usually *love* my birthday. I do. But today, I am nervous. Edgy. I feel prickly and strange. Like everyone is looking at me. I'm unnerved. There's a pit of something odd in my stomach.

It's the same feeling I used to have waking up with a hangover back in my twenties. I'd lie in bed, waiting for the bed to stop spinning. Wondering WHY I ever thought seven cocktails was a good idea. Feeling that same pit of oddness in my belly. In my gut. And I'd wait, every synapse on patrol—*we're on high alert, soldier, this is not a drill*—for the wave of memory to wash over me. To spill over my brain in a cascade of shame as I remembered whatever crazy thing it was I'd done the night before.

I slept with WHO?

I cried WHERE?

I sang WHAT song?

This birthday morning, that's what it feels like. A hangover morning. Except without all the bloaty puffy fun of the cocktails.

I promised myself that I would do WHAT?

Downstairs, wearing a birthday hat made by the kids, I eat cake for breakfast. I consume almost the entire cake by myself. And I do not feel bad about it. The cake is everything to me. I want to have this cake's babies. I savor each bite. I am like a death row inmate having her last meal.

In a text to one of my closest friends that day, I write the following:

"Am going to say yes to anything and everything that scares me. For a whole year. Or until I get scared to death and you have to bury me. Ugh."

My friend writes back:

"Holy crap."

I am not enthusiastic. But I am determined. My logic is wildly simple. It goes like this:

- Saying no has gotten me here.
- Here sucks.
- Saying yes might be my way to someplace better.
- If not a way to someplace better, at least to someplace different.

I didn't have a choice. I didn't *want* a choice. Once I saw the unhappiness, felt the unhappiness, recognized and named it . . . well, just knowing about it made me itchy. Like itchy on the inside of my brain. Continuing to say no was not going to get me anywhere at all. And standing still was no longer an option. The itchy was too much. Besides, I am not a person who can see a problem and *not* solve it.

Before you start to praise me (and frankly, I don't see how you possibly could at this point—but just in case), I want to be clear: I know that I said that I am not a person who can see a problem and not solve it. But I don't mean that in a "heroic Rosa Parks refuses to give up her seat on the bus" way. I mean it in a sad, control-freak, "the toast crusts must be cut off to the same exact millimeter measurement every time" way. Meaning I'm not easygoing about these things.

That's not how I'm built.

That's not how any type A, obsessive, workaholic control freak is built.

Obviously.

I'm a doer.

I do.

So. When I say I'm going to do something, I do it. When I say I'm going to do something, I *really* do it. I throw myself into it and I *do*. I do my *ass* off. I do right up to the finish line. No matter what.

No.

Matter.

What.

This is all made worse by the fact that I'm competitive. Not normal-people competitive. Not friendly competitive. Scary-psychotic competitive. Never hand me a volleyball. Don't ask me to play a fun hand of cards. I have never heard of a casual round of Scrabble. We started a bake-off at *Grey's Anatomy* and I had to remove myself from the competition. Something about it maybe being kind of a little bit like workplace harassment when I forced my writing staff to bake in competition against one another. And maybe it was also not so good when I performed a touchdown dance during the medal ceremony while yelling, "IN YOUR FACE, BITCHES!!!!" at whoever placed behind me.

Like I said, I'm competitive.

I'm not invited to *anyone's* game night.

Look. I'm a person who goes all in.

I lean in. I *lean all the way in*. I lean so far in that sometimes I'm lying down.

Hell, I don't own Thursday nights for *nothing*.

I tell you this so that you understand how big this yes-for-a-year thing was for me. This Year of Yes thing was gigantic. The Year of Yes promise was a commitment. A binding contract between me and my greatest competitor and judge—me. Backing out would mean months of self-flagellation and plummeting self-esteem. I would talk about me like a *dog*. Things would get ugly.

Also, honestly?

I was just . . . desperate.

Something had to change. It had to. Because this couldn't be it.

Having it all.

This could not possibly be what having it all was supposed to feel like. Could it? Because if it was, if *this* is what I spent all this time and energy working so hard for, if this was what the promised land looked like, was what success felt like, was what I sacrificed for . . .

I didn't even want to consider it. So I wouldn't. I would not think about that. Instead, I would look ahead, take a deep breath and just . . . believe. Believe that the road continued. Believe that there was more.

I would believe and I would say yes.

I told myself that and then I ate that whole cake and drank four mimosas while trying to believe.

yesyesyesyesyesyesyesyesyesyesyesyesyesyesyesyes

A week later, the phone rings at my Shondaland office. President Hanlon from Dartmouth College is calling. College presidents do not make it a habit to telephone me. I have met President Hanlon, a very nice man, exactly once. Nevertheless, here he is, President Hanlon of Dartmouth College, on my phone. Calling. He has a question. He wants to know if I will give the commencement speech at the college's graduation in June.

A twenty-minute speech. In front of about ten thousand people.

Ummm.

Universe?

Are you freaking kidding me?

There is an actual full minute that occurs on that phone call in which no air moves in or out of my lungs. President Hanlon may or may not be speaking. I do not know because the roar in my ears is making it impossible for me to hear.

Say yes to everything for a year.

This is it. It's happening. And now that it is here, saying yes stops being just a vague idea. Now the reality of what I am embarking upon sends my brain thundering around inside of my skull.

Say yes?

There's no way to plan. There's no way to hide. There's no way to control this. Not if I am saying yes to everything.

Yes to everything scary.

Yes to everything that takes me out of my comfort zone.

Yes to everything that feels like it might be crazy.

Yes to everything that feels out of character.

Yes to everything that feels goofy.

Yes to everything.

Everything.

Say yes.

Yes.

Speak. Speak NOW.

"Yes," I say. "Yes."

President Hanlon and I chat some more. I think it's pleasant. I think I'm calm. I really have no idea. I am focused on breathing in and out. On lowering the roar I hear. When I hang up the phone, I consider what I've done.

Speech. Commencement. Ten thousand people.

I input the date into my calendar.

June 8, 2014.

June.

That's about six months away. Six months is pretty far off.

Six months is a *lifetime*.

Okay. I shrug and go back to writing my *Grey's Anatomy* script notes.

Relieved. Not a big deal. I'll think about it later.

I file it away in the back of my brain and forget about it. I forget about it for *five and a half months*. You'd think that would be bad, given the giant speech I have to write. But instead, it turns out to be lucky. It turns out that I have other hurdles.

The Dartmouth commencement speech is technically my first yes.

Really, though?

The Dartmouth commencement speech is the first thing I say yes *to*. But it's not the first yes that I actually have to DO.

That's a different yes. And that yes? Turned out to be something much more terrifying.

Hello, Jimmy Kimmel.

4

Yes to the Sun

"They want you to be on *Kimmel*."

My publicist, Chris DiIorio, is talking to me.

Yeah, I have a publicist. A publicist sounds like an "I'm on the cover of *Vogue*" kind of thing to have. The kind of thing you have if you are luminous like Jennifer Lawrence or stop traffic every time you move like Lupita Nyong'o.

As I write this, my hair is standing straight up on my head because it's been a few days since I combed it and I'm wearing a pair of pajamas where the top and bottom do not match. They're not even the same fabric. The bottoms are silky, the top is stretch knit. There's a hole in the knee of the pajamas. Hello, *Vogue*. Yeah, I have a publicist.

When I first got a publicist, I told him and his team that my main reason for having a publicist was so that I never ever had to do any publicity. Everyone thought this was a joke. I was not joking.

It seems, being that everyone around me knows that I am awkward, introverted and visibly uncomfortable when meeting new people, that it would be kinda obvious that I would be panicked at the thought of standing on a stage talking to an audience, having my photo taken by a horde of photographers, being on TV, making public appearances of any kind, really.

You'd get that it would probably not be my favorite thing, right? You would, gentle reader, wouldn't you?

That is because you don't work in Hollywood.

In Hollywood, it is assumed that a person would be excited about a spotlight shining right on their face while they sat on a toilet on live TV.

I joke, right? No, still not joking.

Seriously. I think, given the chance, there are plenty of people in Hollywood who would LINE UP to do it. They'd line up for a casting session that read "PERSON ON TOILET."

Why? WHY?

For the exposure. For the *endorsement* opportunity.

"I could have my own line of toilets, you never know," they'd say, and plop right down on that porcelain throne.

When I meet you, let's hold hands and weep for humanity, okay?

The terrifying existence of willing public-toilet-sitters in this town is why my publicist, Chris, is genuinely confused when I say I never want any publicity. He tells me that I will change my mind.

In the words of the greatest singer ever, Whitney Houston, on the greatest reality show that ever was, *Being Bobby Brown*: "*Hell to the naw.*"

Even if I *was* Beyoncé, even if I woke up like *that*? I would still prefer to stay hidden. I would still want to quietly write scripts back there in the corner where no one could see me. I *never* want anyone looking at me. Being looked at makes me nervous.

When I am required by ABC to do publicity, I often feel (and, sadly, look) like Bambi's mother—right before the hunter shoots her. Her head snapped up, ears cocked, eyes wide, all freaked out . . .

It's not an attractive look.

At Dartmouth, I acted in some plays for a student theater group named BUTA. I enjoyed it. I sort of reveled in it. I was even mildly decent at it. I got compliments. But I wasn't me. I never had to step in front of an audience as Shonda Rhimes. My own words and thoughts were not needed. I just said whatever Ntozake Shange or George C. Wolfe or Shakespeare told me to say. No one was looking at *me*. They were looking through me to the writers. I never felt I was visible onstage.

Back then, I had fun in front of an audience. But now? It

didn't matter the venue or the medium. Now, it was always akin to torture. And season after season, the TCAs were a prime torture method.

Every year, twice a year, all the cable and network channels host a weeklong event for TV critics called, quite simply, TCAs. It's a chance for the critics to talk to actors, showrunners, directors. More times than I can count, ABC has requested my presence on a TCA panel.

Onstage doing a panel at TCAs, I know I always looked fine. In fact, I looked stern—like a scolding schoolmarm. I've seen all the photos. I'm frowning, stony. I am actually amazed by my face's ability to not betray my inner turmoil. The extreme fear seemed to freeze my face, turning me into a statue to protect me while onstage.

But beforehand, every single time, before I got to the stage . . . there was mumbling, there was sweating, there was shaking. There was the makeup artist charged with reapplying the mascara that washed off my face after the silent thirty-second crying jag required to quell my rising hysteria. There were executives from ABC who gathered around to say encouraging things as I paced back and forth, my glassy eyeballs spinning with fear. And then there was the exquisite bottle of red wine always given to me by the network president, who owned a vineyard. Because I never *ever* spoke in public without two glasses of wine in my system. Nature's beta blocker.

I am not saying that it was right.

I am saying that it *worked*.

My only good memory of sitting on that TCA stage was the year *Desperate Housewives* creator Marc Cherry very kindly took pity on me during a showrunners' panel. As a storm of questions about an unhappy actress came my way, he jumped in, answering and deflecting the worst of them with a series of amazing jokes. Twenty minutes before, someone— I don't remember who—had been forced to pry my fingers off the door handle of my car to get me inside. I hadn't been resisting. I'd just been frozen by fear and unable to move.

I was a walking panic attack. My stage fright was so complete and overwhelming that it ruled my every public appearance. Award acceptance speeches, interviews, talk shows . . . Oprah.

Oprah.

I have been interviewed by Oprah three times.

Here is what I remember about being interviewed by Oprah.

A white-hot flashing light behind my eyes. A strange numbness in my limbs. A high-pitched buzzing sound in my head.

So, y'know . . . nothing.

NOTHING.

I am from the suburbs of Chicago. I was *raised* on Oprah. I was watching *The Oprah Winfrey Show* when it was called

AM Chicago. I bought everything she told us to buy and read every book she told us to read. I took notes on every word of wisdom she shared with us through the television. I was baptized Catholic but I was Church of Oprah. If you are a person on the planet, you know what I am talking about. Everybody knows. It's OPRAH.

Being interviewed by Oprah was no small thing for me.

What do I remember about these precious moments spent with her?

Nothing.

The *O* magazine interview? Nothing.

The Oprah show interview with the cast of *Grey's Anatomy*? Zilch.

The *Oprah's Next Chapter* interview with Kerry Washington? Not a damn thing.

I do have vivid memories of the moments just *before* these interviews. That first time, *Grey's* costume designer Mimi Melgaard smoothed my skirt and spun me around, checking to make sure I looked okay. Then she nodded with approval and pointed a firm finger at me.

"Do not move until you see Oprah."

She didn't have to tell me that.

I couldn't have moved if I'd wanted to. I stood in the doorway of my office. Swaying very slightly back and forth. My feet already hurting in their very first pair of Manolo Blahniks.

My mind was as blank as a baby chicken.

I felt a layer of sweat wash over me. *Sweat.* Robotically, I began raising and lowering my arms, hoping to keep giant circular pit stains from appearing and ruining all of Mimi's Pygmalion work.

Raise and lower, raise and lower, raise and lower . . .

Flapping. I was flapping my arms.

Now I looked like a baby chicken.

It didn't matter. The rising terror thundering through me was growing louder and louder, taking me somewhere so far past fear that I felt almost . . . serene. It was like listening to a sound so high-pitched that your eardrums cease to be able to process it and the sound becomes silent. My screaming fear was so loud that it was silent.

The baby chicken was losing its head.

I watched as Oprah's black SUV rumbled onto the studio lot. I watched as Oprah's black SUV rolled into the VIP parking space. I watched as first one woman and then a second woman climbed from the black SUV. The first woman so recognizable, so familiar, that I literally only had to see the tip of her foot hitting the ground to know—it was Oprah. But the second woman . . . still flapping my sweaty arms, I stared. I couldn't identify the second woman. Who was it?

And then the arm flapping stopped.

Gayle, my brain realized. *That is Gayle. Sweet Mother of Television, I am looking at both Oprah AND Gayle.*

And that is the last thing I remember before the nothingness of terror stole all the fun away from me.

"How was it?" My sisters Sandie and Delorse grilled me breathlessly on the phone later that evening. The ONE time I managed to impress my sisters. The one time, and—

I. Don't. Know.

That is *not* what I said.

Have you learned nothing about me since starting this book? No, you have. You know me. You *know*.

I'm old. And I like to lie.

I did what I'd always done. Once Oprah got back in her SUV and drove away, I spent hours wandering around, casually asking anyone who'd witnessed even a second of Oprahness all about it. Getting them to recap what they saw. It was a coping mechanism that had always worked for me. I was careful about it. Because when you go around asking people to tell you about yourself, you sound like kind of a jerk.

"Hey, tell me what I said. What was I like? Was I funny? Was I interesting? Tell me more about me talking to Oprah. Was it good?"

It's one thing for people to know you are nervous and have stage fright. They are sympathetic to that. But how do you admit to people that you don't remember the biggest interview of your career? That is weird. You know what people would say about that? I'll tell you. People would say:

Drugs.

So I kept my mouth shut.

It was the worst with Oprah. My admiration and fear merged into some sort of fireball of terror, so that the paintings were not just stolen off the walls of my brain but burned down to a heap of ashes. Never to be recovered.

With everyone else, I stood a chance. A small chance. But to some degree, all the interviewers were scary. Every talk show was a blur. Every interview went the same way. Down the drain.

yesyesyesyesyesyesyesyesyesyesyesyesyesyesyesyes

I've been asked to be on *Kimmel* before.

It makes sense that Jimmy Kimmel would want people from my shows on his show. Because of the ratings. My TGIT shows (that's how ABC promotes my Thursday night lineup of shows—"Thank God It's Thursday") get good ratings. Good ratings are good for everyone. Here's why: my good ratings mean that when actors who star on my shows are guests on *Jimmy Kimmel Live* (also on ABC), it's great for Jimmy's ratings too. What's great for us is great for Jimmy.

This is what is called *synergy*. I know this because people say this word to me a lot. Then they give me meaningful looks.

"Synergy." Meaningful look. I nod and smile, but between you and me? I think *synergy* sounds like the word one uses to define the calories two people burn off during sex.

Think about it.

*Syn*ergy.

Anyway.

It turns out that Jimmy, who is a truly hilarious person, a very nice guy and a great talk show host, doesn't just like us for our ratings. He actually really likes our shows. I *think* he does anyway. He definitely likes the casts of our shows. This year, he especially seems to love the cast of *Scandal*. Which is just fine because the cast of *Scandal* loves Jimmy and they enjoy being on his show.

And so each Thursday, actors like Kerry Washington and Katie Lowes get dressed up and pay Jimmy and his studio audience a visit. They come back and tell me stories. They tell me how much fun it is to be on Jimmy's show. They tell me about the skits they do. The pranks they pull. The jokes they tell. It sounds fun. And when I watch it all on *Jimmy Kimmel Live* on TV late at night, it LOOKS fun.

Yay for everyone!

But for some reason, Jimmy now wants something more. For some reason, he wants me to be a guest on his show.

Jimmy likes this idea.

ABC likes this idea.

My publicist likes this idea.

I do not like this idea.

No one cares.

No one *believes* me.

Because who doesn't want to be on TV?

Quick, everyone climb on that toilet and roll camera!

This year, Jimmy's people (every show has "people"—Kimmel's are extraordinarily nice) have asked a few times if I will be a guest on his show.

"They want you to be on *Kimmel.*"

My publicist, Chris. Talking to me. We're on the phone. Which is lucky for me because of the jail time that comes with assault.

"You mean," I say tightly, "*Jimmy Kimmel LIVE.*"

"Uh-huh." He sounds nonchalant. Casual. But he knows.

He knows how I feel about publicity. He knows how I feel about being interviewed. He knows how I feel about being interviewed on TV. And he especially knows how I feel about *live* TV.

You know what happens on live TV?

Janet Jackson's Super Bowl Boob happens on live TV. Adele Dazeem happens on live TV. President Al Gore happens on live TV.

You know what else happens on live TV?

Shonda walking out to greet Jimmy and instead of walking like a *normal* person, I trip over my own feet, falling and cracking my head on the corner of Jimmy's desk, causing my cerebrospinal fluid to leak out as I lie twitching on the ground with my dress bunched up around my waist, revealing my double Spanx to a national audience.

Shonda, under the hot lights of the studio and massively overcome by nerves, sweating so profusely that tsunamis of water roll down my face in a hideous but fascinating car-crash way that no one can look away from until finally, dehydrated from the water loss, I simply end the misery by fainting on the floor in front of Jimmy's desk.

Shonda doing what I did at my U Penn applicant mixer when the stuffy old host said, "I'm not going to give you a lot of *buffalo* about our school . . ." What did I do? What I did was, surrounded by a lot of prep school kids with blond hair and perfect clothes, burst into loud uncontrollable snorting howling laughter. (Needless to say, I did not attend U Penn. Don't smirk. I got in. But I couldn't go there. One of those rich blond kids was gonna see me on campus and tell everyone about the snorting howling laughter.) I do that when I'm nervous. So imagine what it would be like when I'm *extremely* nervous. Live. With Jimmy.

Shonda bursting into loud uncontrollable snorting howling laughter at Jimmy's very first joke, laughter and snorting that gets louder and louder and louder, laughter that I know CANNOT BE STOPPED, that I have no *chance* of stopping despite the absurdity of laughing hysterically in front of Jimmy and Jimmy's live studio audience, a fact which makes me scream with laughter, louder and louder, harder and harder—until the hiccups come.

You can die from the hiccups. For real. I'm a fake doctor

who writes fake medicine for TV. So I know stuff. And I am telling you, we killed Meredith's stepmother with hiccups and that could happen to me. I could laugh until I hiccup and hiccup and die. I could DIE on live TV. Literally die. Do you want me to do that to Jimmy? Do you want me to make Jimmy the guy who killed a guest? I think not.

You know what else you don't want to see?

Shonda having spontaneous fear-snot shoot out of my face.

Fear-snot.

Nuff said.

All of these things could happen if I were to go on live TV. These are all *not* good things. These are bad things. Baaaaaaad things.

You may think I'm exaggerating. Or trying to be funny.

Does fear-snot sound funny to you? Close your eyes and imagine it shooting out of your face in front of twelve million people. It's not funny. It's not funny at all.

Okay, I have never had fear-snot. But I am the kind of person who WOULD GET fear-snot. It would happen to me. Simply because it would be horrifying. That is how the universe likes to treat me, teach me, keep me in line. I'm the girl who splits her pants and does not notice the breeze. I'm the woman who forgets to cut the price tag off my dress and walks around with it stuck to my back so everyone can see not only how much I spent but also WHAT SIZE I AM for an entire dinner party. I'm the one who spills. Who trips. Who drops. I once accidentally flung a chicken bone across the room at a very elegant cocktail party while trying to make a point.

Did you hear me?

I FLUNG A CHICKEN BONE ACROSS THE ROOM AT A COCKTAIL PARTY.

While everyone stared at the chicken bone on the white carpet, I pretended that the culprit was not me. True story.

You can't take me anywhere.

You certainly can't take me somewhere and then film me live in front of millions of people. Because if there is fear-snot to be had, I WILL HAVE IT.

And Chris knows this. He knows what could happen on live TV. He knows how I feel about live TV.

He just doesn't care.

He doesn't have time for fear-snot. He's trying to help me build a career here.

Against my will.

Over the years, every single time that Kimmel's people have asked me to be a guest on *Jimmy Kimmel Live*, I've said no.

And no.

And no.

I don't tell Kimmel's people that I am saying no because live TV is a minefield. I don't tell them that I am saying no because I am afraid I may accidentally Janet Jackson Boob Jimmy. Or pee on his sofa like an excited puppy. Or fall on my face before I even make it to the sofa. Or die. I don't say anything about any of that.

Because I'm a lady, damn it.

I just say no.

Kimmel's people are so nice. When I see them at ABC events, they smile at me while I look at them with my statue face and my swirly eyeballs.

Then I shuffle to the buffet table to put some food on top of my stress.

I am pretty sure that the super-nice Kimmel people think I'm an asshole.

My publicist, Chris, doesn't think I'm an asshole. He thinks I am a pain in the ass. To him, I am the Sisyphean ball he has been shoving up this same hill for years now. And yet he continues to believe. He continues to hope.

He keeps hope *alive*.

He uses buzzwords. Buzzwords we both know I can't just say no to. They want to do an *hour-long* Scandal *special*. On *finale* night. *ABC is excited*. And it's a delicate time for me and ABC right now. So I have to be a team player. If I say no, I am not being a good team player. All that Athlete Talk will have been for nothing.

See, I am in the middle of negotiations for my next contract.

You understand what I'm saying?

Athlete Talk has to MEAN something.

We sit on the phone together. I am silent. I'm hoping he'll get the hint, hang up and call ABC and tell them I have the plague. It could happen. I could get the plague. I feel it coming on right now.

Chris doesn't hang up. He never hangs up.

He's silent.

He's waiting me out. This is a contest we engage in frequently. Finally, as always, I speak first.

"I do not want to be on television. Ever," I remind him. "Never. Ever. For any reason. No one needs to see me. Why would anyone need to see me when they could be seeing Kerry Washington?"

I believe this deeply. Have you seen Kerry Washington? Kerry Washington is extraordinary.

"Kerry Washington just had a baby," Chris reminds me.

Right. Kerry is quite rightly taking some much-needed bonding time with her new baby. Mother to mother, I feel solidarity with her on that. Damn.

"Tony then! Or Bellamy! Bellamy is amazing!"

I start calling out the names of *Scandal* actors. Chris takes a deep breath. Then he lists all the reasons why I should be on TV. These reasons make no sense to me. He may as well be speaking German. Because I don't speak German. Or that really cool Khoisan language in Namibia that is just a series of clicks.

"I do not understand a thing you are saying!" I holler.

"Why would I want to be *more* recognizable? That is the exact opposite of what I want to be!! Make this go away!"

Chris is now likely contemplating whether it will be more satisfying to sew a suit made out of my skin or to simply scatter the chopped-up pieces of my corpse in the ocean.

Maybe he's just thinking about hobbling me, Stephen King *Misery*—style.

I wouldn't blame him. I'd fight him, but I wouldn't blame him. I mean, I am screaming at him. I am actually screaming at him in a hysterical voice. Fear is taking over. I'm losing it. I can *feel* myself losing it and a part of me wants to hobble me too. Because, dude: when you become a person with any kind of power, don't ever become a person who screams. Even in hysterical fear.

The things that you can do when you are at the bottom of the ladder change as you move up. At the top of that ladder, doing many of those very same things makes you an asshole. I'm being an asshole. A very scared, very shy asshole.

Chris is quiet for a long, long, long moment.

He's going to place my head in a box like that guy did to Brad Pitt's girlfriend in *Seven*. I know it. I don't want my head in a box. My head will not look good in a box. I listen nervously to the silence.

But when he speaks, his voice has the calm tone of power and triumph.

He's going to win. And he knows it.

Here's why:

"Shonda," he says, "I thought you were saying yes to everything. Or was that just big talk?"

Damn.

Checkmate.

Maybe I can put *his* head in a box.

yesyesyesyesyesyesyesyesyesyesyesyesyesyesyesyesyes

I thought saying YES would feel good. I thought it would feel freeing. Like Julie Andrews spinning around on that big mountaintop at the beginning of *The Sound of Music*. Like Angela Bassett when she's Tina Turner and she walks out of that divorce court and away from Ike with nothing but her name in *What's Love Got to Do with It*. Like how you feel when you have just finished baking double-fudge brownies but you have yet to shove one into your mouth, starting the sugar rush roller coaster that won't end until you are curled up in a ball on the sofa, rocking back and forth while scraping the crumbs of the empty brownie pan into your mouth and trying to talk yourself into believing that maybe the ex-boyfriend you dumped wasn't so bad after all.

Like that.

This *YES* does not feel like a post-baked, pre-eaten brownie.

I feel forced into this. I feel like I don't have a choice. My obligation to my network plus my obligation to my stupid Year of Yes idea has trapped me.

My paw is caught in a trap. I can try to chew it off and run away. But if you think I am whining now? Try me when I'm down a paw and have just a bloody gnawed stump to deal with.

The tears.

The drama.

The wailing and moaning.

The cross I would be nailing myself to would be so pretty and brightly lit. Oh, my cross wouldn't be missed by anyone! You'd see my cross from space.

The numbing fear is starting to creep over me. This is going to be a terrible experience. It's going to eat me alive. My left eye starts to twitch. I tell myself that it's okay, because it is twitching only in what I am sure is the tiniest, most unnoticeable way. Nobody can tell it is twitching but me.

"Wow, your eye is really twitching," Joan Rater, head writer at *Grey's Anatomy,* informs me with great authority. The whole writing staff crowds around to peer at my eyeball jumping around in my head.

"Honey," my toddler, Emerson, takes my face in her hands and gravely informs me, "your eye is broken. It's busted, honey."

This is not going to be okay.

This is not what *YES* is supposed to feel like.

If it is, this is going to be the longest year of my life.

Later that same week, I'm sitting on the soundstage at *Grey's Anatomy*. Cranky as hell. It is not enough that my eyeball is still twitching merrily away. It's Season Ten. Sandra Oh is leaving the show. As we move closer to her final episode, every scene with her begins to feel more and more special. We are all very aware that a rare talent is soon going to be walking out the door. I've come to set for the rehearsal of a big scene.

To help close out Cristina's story line, Isaiah Washington has returned to do us the honor and favor of scrubbing in as Preston Burke. Right now, in this scene, Preston is telling Cristina that he is giving her his hospital—like Willy Wonka giving away the Chocolate Factory. It's the biggest moment of the show for Cristina, the culmination of ten seasons of character growth. She stands face-to-face with the man she almost destroyed herself loving. She'd once lost herself in his orbit, revolving around him, desperately in need of his sun. She'd made herself smaller to accommodate his greatness. Now she has surpassed him. And he is paying his respects. He has come to praise her. The Chocolate Factory is hers if she wants it.

One half of the Twisted Sisters is getting her fairy-tale ending: she's being offered what she has earned, she's being recognized for her brilliance and she is being rewarded with her dreams come true. It may not be the fairy-tale ending anyone else would want or would want *for* her, but Cristina does not give a damn. Frankly, neither do I. Cristina deserves her joy.

This is what joy looks like to a woman with genius.

And as I watch Sandra Oh's face tell a whole story as she brilliantly gives nuance to the moment Cristina realizes Burke is handing her the keys to the kingdom, I realize why Cristina's journey can end. I realize why it is time to let this character go and be happy for her.

Cristina has learned what she needs to know. Her toolbox is full. She has learned to not let go of the pieces of herself that she needs in order to be what someone else wants. She's learned not to compromise. She's learned not to settle. She's learned, as difficult as it is, how to be her own sun.

If only real life were so simple.

But my eye stops twitching.

And I pick up the phone and I call Chris.

"Janet Jackson Boob," I tell him. "Fear-snot. Chicken bone."

There's a long silence while Chris perhaps worries that I have had a stroke.

"Huh?"

"It can't be live. I will do *Jimmy Kimmel*. But it can't be live," I say firmly.

I can hear Chris breathing in and out. He's going to eat my kidney and liver with a fine wine.

"Let me get this straight," he says tightly. "You will be on *Jimmy Kimmel LIVE*. As long as it is not LIVE."

He says this as if speaking to a crazy person. And maybe he is.

But I just watched Cristina Yang get her Chocolate Factory. I'm feeling bold. I'm not compromising. I don't need to settle.

"Exactly," I tell him.

If I have to be on TV, if I have to do something as scary as *Kimmel*, we're going to do it my way or we don't do it at all.

See, I'm keeping all my pieces.

I don't want brownies.

I want a whole damn Chocolate Factory.

YES should feel like the sun.

yesyesyesyesyesyesyesyesyesyesyesyesyesyesyesyes

I have no idea how it happened or what conversations took place or whose baby he had to steal or what favor I now owe to what stranger or which warlord I am now betrothed to.

I do not know. And I do not care.

Chris did it.

The man made rain.

Which is how, the week before the *Scandal* finale aired, I found myself sitting on the set of Pope & Associates with Jimmy Kimmel filming an hour-long *not*-live special called *Jimmy Kimmel Live: Behind the Scandalabra*.

Jimmy was incredibly nice to me. He told me funny stories and asked me about my children while we waited for the
camera to roll. Before every take he patiently told me what
was going to happen next and then he told me the very same
thing *again*, like he knew I had the brain of a very demented
senior citizen who could only remember two or three words
at a time. He kept asking me if I was okay. And if he thought
it was weird that I became a block of solid wood and could
not seem to both walk and talk while the camera was rolling,
he kept it to himself. He simply arranged it so I never had to
walk and talk at the same time. In fact, he made it so I barely
had to talk. I'm serious. Go online. Watch it. What am I doing?

1. Smiling.
2. Trying really hard not to look directly into the camera.
3. Laughing at Jimmy's jokes.
4. Holding a really big glass while Scott Foley pours wine
   into it.
5. Looking directly into the camera even though I've been
   told not to A LOT.
6. Laughing at Jimmy's jokes some more.

Jimmy did *all* the work. I didn't have to do anything. And
yet. He made it SEEM like I did stuff. Everyone thought I
did all kinds of stuff. So he did all the work and I got all the
credit.

Like when a baby poops.

Everyone fawns over the baby. Now, who is the one cleaning up the poop? *Not* the baby, I can tell you that. But no one is fawning over the person carrying that smelly diaper to the trash.

I think I just likened myself to a pooping baby. But you get my point. Jimmy did all kinds of amazing things to make me look good. And because Jimmy does his show all the time and is always amazing, everyone just nodded and smiled at him. But because there was a very good chance that there would be fear-snot and chicken bones surrounding me, I got a standing ovation from everyone I know.

I got calls. I got emails. I got tweets and facebooks and all the other social media things people get.

The next day, I also got the biggest delivery of red roses ever.

EVER.

Like "horse winning the Kentucky Derby" big.

They came in a giant silver vase. A vase so huge and heavy that it took three men to carry it into the house. My daughter Harper tried counting the red roses but lost interest after ninety-eight.

The dozens and dozens of red roses were from Jimmy.

He wasn't proposing marriage.

The ratings had come out. *Jimmy Kimmel Live* beat *The*

Tonight Show Starring Jimmy Fallon for the very first time ever with that episode.

That was the nicest thing.

Kimmel beat Fallon. Which meant Kimmel was right to keep asking me to be on the show. And Chris was right to force me to do it. And I guess I was right to ask that it be taped. Because I do not know if the results would have been the same if I'd been unable to come out on live TV because I was having a full-scale meltdown in the corner of the *Jimmy Kimmel Live* dressing room.

But none of that mattered to me. Not really. I mean, I was grateful that Jimmy was happy. I was grateful that I hadn't messed up one of his shows. But overwhelmingly, I could only think about one thing:

I did it.

I said yes to something that terrified me. And then I did it.

And I didn't die.

There's a crack in the pantry door. A sliver of light coming in. I can feel a bit of warm sun on my face.

I wander over to Chris.

"Thank you," I mumble.

"What? I didn't hear you."

"THANK YOU."

Chris grins. Triumphant.

He heard me the first time. You know he did. I know he did. We ALL know he did. But I don't mind.

Fear-snot. Chicken bone. Adele Dazeem.

What do I care? It *happened*. I did it.

And I kept all my pieces.

YES does feel like the sun.

Maybe I'm building my own damn Chocolate Factory.

5

Yes to Speaking the Whole Truth

Early in 2014, I'm invited to join a small private women's online network. It quickly becomes a lifeline for me. It's full of smart women who do interesting things, and I look forward to its missives. Fascinating conversations fly back and forth all day over email. New to the group, I mind my Ps and Qs and keep my mouth shut. I'm an observer, a listener. I wander on the outskirts. Rarely do I consider even joining the conversation.

On May 29, about a week and a half before I am due to stand at the podium at Dartmouth College and deliver the required twenty-to-thirty-minute commencement address to an audience of what is now a roughly estimated sixteen thousand people, I write the following email to the group:

FROM: Shonda

TO: The Group

RE: My Death

So it's happening soon. My commencement speech. And (shocker!) I haven't written a word. I got totally paralyzed. The paralyzing moment happened when I was brushing my teeth and listening to NPR and heard someone on there (someone I love and admire) say that one of the speeches they were most looking forward to discussing was . . . mine.

No pressure. No pressure at all.

Apparently now, these speeches are filmed and streamed and uploaded and tweeted and dissected and NPR has a WHOLE site dedicated to dissecting them.

People don't faint when they give these speeches, right? That has not happened?

Do you see what I said there?
I said that I have not written a word.
And it is true. Less than two weeks from the day.
I have not written a word.
NOT ONE SINGLE WORD.
I wander around feeling white-hot terror searing all cre-

ativity out of my brain. The fires of failure are whipping around, burning down any ideas I may have had.

It's a writing apocalypse up in my imagination.

I lie on the floor of my office. I drink red wine. I eat popcorn. I hug my kids. I prepare for the end of days.

Every work email I write in those ten days before the speech says basically the same thing: *Why are you asking me whatever thing you are asking me? Don't you know I am about to die of humiliation and fear while giving a speech? Let me have this time to say good-bye to my family!*

I become nonsensical. Irrational. I stop speaking out loud. I make noises instead.

"Grmmph," I say to my assistant, Abby, when she asks me if I would like to take a certain meeting.

"Bllummppth," I mutter to the writers when they ask if I have any story ideas.

The women in my online network send me words of support. They send advice. They remind me to power pose.

"Power pose like Wonder Woman!"

Power posing like Wonder Woman is when you stand up like a badass—legs in a wide stance, chin up, hands on your hips. Like you own the place. Like you have on magical silver bracelets and know how to use them. Like your superhero cape is flapping in the wind behind you.

I'm not just some dork telling you to pretend to be Wonder Woman.

It's a real thing.

My online network tells me to power pose like Wonder Woman and reminds me of the actual studies that say that power posing like Wonder Woman for five minutes not only improves self-esteem but even hours later improves how others perceive you.

Let me say that again.

Standing around like Wonder Woman in the morning can make people think you are more amazing at lunchtime.

Crazy. But true.

How awesome is that?

(You don't believe me? Watch the TED Talk.)

I start power posing every time I step into an elevator. It makes for some awkward rides up and down with strangers. But I soldier on. I'll take whatever help I can get.

More wisdom comes in. One of the women writes with this helpful gem: she wants me to remember that the worst thing that can happen to me is that I'll crap my pants onstage. As long as that doesn't happen, she instructs me, I'll be fine.

Surprisingly, this pants-crapping information somehow makes me feel better. Calmer. Because crapping my pants is not a thing I do. My certainty on this matter makes it possible for me to sleep at night. It also allows me to begin writing bits and pieces of my speech. Which I do on little scraps of paper that I continuously lose. I switch to the Notes app on my phone.

But even as it comes together, I'm not sure the speech is any good. And I don't really have time to think about it. I've just finished producing forty-two episodes of television. It's the fewest number of episodes that I've produced in a long time for any given TV season—but still, I'm bone tired. *Private Practice* took its bow the season before, so I've lost a show. But I've added a child. A CHILD. An actual person, a tiny human. Thankfully, Kerry Washington has added one too and I praise the heavens for the gift of only eighteen episodes of *Scandal* this season. I say it aloud to no one but I'm not sure I could have coped with more. Keeping up with three children, sleeping, working, writing and trying to do it all well has been kicking my ass lately. By that moment in June, I was feeling pretty low about my Mommy Scorecard.

The Mommy Scorecard is a thing I keep in my head. On it is an imaginary series of zeros and tens that get dished out by some imaginary judge-y bitch who looks an awful lot like me. The zeros hit the card when I fail: when I miss a recital because I'm traveling, when I forget that it's my turn to provide food for preschool snack day, when we don't make it to a birthday party because the introvert in me just can't face the magnitude of all the social interaction.

I keep hearing about these Mommy Wars. Debates are raging: which child-rearing style is best, what makes a bad mother, who is to blame for kids with "problems," how involved should you be at the school—it goes on and on. Really, it comes down to this: which kind of mother is screwing up her kid more? People love to talk about these Mommy Wars all the time in magazines. Talk show hosts plead: can't we all come together? But I never really got what everyone was talking about.

The only mommy I am ever at war with is me.

It doesn't help that I now have a tween—a glorious, lanky, stunningly beautiful, future supermodel of a tween—who, like all tweens, possesses a special skill for twisting the knife I've already firmly implanted in my own chest.

"This is the third recital you've missed," she'll remind me. "And . . . are you ever coming to one of my science fairs?"

It's *not* the third recital. And I was just at the science fair last quarter. But she makes it sound like I wasn't. Which makes me feel like I wasn't.

Boom.

A zero.

Now, I'm no fool. I'm not one of those mothers who allows her children to behave like monsters and walk all over me.

I was raised old-school.

I strive to be old-school.

My kids are not my friends. They are my children. My goal is not to get them to like me. My goal is to raise citizens. My world does not revolve around them. The only helicopter in my life is the toy helicopter that the kids play with.

So my response to my daughter Harper isn't a wringing of my hands and a tearful apology. Nobody did any hand-wringing and apologizing while raising me and I turned out . . . a *writer*.

"I work to feed and clothe you. Do you want food and clothes? Then be quiet and show some gratitude."

That is what I say to my tween.

But inside? Zero on the Mommy Scorecard. Knife twisted a little more. And the commencement speech . . . I have less and less time to focus on it, to obsess about it, to worry over it. It's the end of the season, it's the end of the school year.

The day I'm due to fly to Hanover, New Hampshire, I spend the early morning with my youngest daughters. Then I head over to my tween's school to attend the end-of-the-year ceremony. My daughter is receiving an academic award and, while I already know this, she does not. I don't want to miss seeing her face when she finds out. I arrive just in time to see her name called and, as her face lights up, I attack her with my camera for photos. There are hugs, smiles, joy. And though I have reminded her every day for weeks, there is the inevitable disappointed face when she hears me say I need to leave. Knife twisting again, I rush off to the airport.

It's not until I'm on the plane, away from my real life and surrounded by the close friends I've brought with me for support, that I really look at the speech I've written. That I really face it.

For a while, I feel sick. A cold, hard rock settles at the bottom of my stomach. It's the same kind of speech I have always written. Pithy, witty, snappy. It has highs and lows. Jokes. It's smart and shiny. And it sounds just fine. Except I'm not actually saying anything. I'm not revealing anything. I'm not sharing anything. There is nothing of *me* in here. I speak from behind a curtain. It's like a magic trick—I open my mouth but you never actually hear *me*. You just hear my voice. This speech is all Athlete Talk.

I imagine standing up at that podium tomorrow and looking into the faces of those graduates and . . . What? If I say nothing of substance, tell them nothing, share nothing, give nothing . . . why? Why am I even there?

What am I afraid they will see if I am really myself?

I know it's not the graduates. It's the rest of the world. It's all the other people out there who will hear the speech and judge it and criticize it. And know things about me because of it. I don't know if I want them to know me. Because . . . because . . . I still don't truly know me.

What I do know is that I cannot deliver this speech.

I know that I will not deliver this speech.

This speech is not a *YES*.

I read through it four or five more times. Then I tuck it away into a new folder on my laptop. I label the folder CRAP.

And then I start over.

What I write next is less formal, less stuffy, less stylized.

What I write is casual and a little raw and sometimes inappropriate.

But it's honest.

And it sounds like me.

It *is* me.

If I'm going to give a speech, if I'm going to stand up there and give a speech in front of all these people, if I'm going to make this leap . . .

. . . if I'm going to say yes . . .

If I am going to say YES . . .

I might as well say yes to being me.

No Athlete Talk.

No magic tricks.

I just tell the truth.

When I am done, as the plane streaks through the night sky, I hit Save. And I promise myself that I won't think about the speech too much more until I am standing at the podium.

The morning of graduation I am up before dawn. I need to jump up and down. Stretch. Breathe. I spend more than a few moments Power Posing. From the window of my suite at the Hanover Inn, I can see the stage. I can see the traditional Old Pine Lectern that serves as the podium from which I am to speak.

I stare at it for a long time in the sunrise.

I am going to say yes to everything that scares me.

I wait for the wave of fear and panic to wash over me. But it doesn't come. I shrug to myself. It'll be here any minute, I know. I'm tense, waiting for it. Any second, the familiar freezing panic of stage fright will hit me. The tsunami will hit me.

But it never does.

I am nervous. I am scared. But that is all.

The next few hours are a whirlwind. Photos. Gowns and caps. Shaking lots of hands. Waves of nostalgia. And I keep waiting for the attack of nerves that usually renders me useless. That causes me to become a sweaty pile of hyperventilation. I wait as we march to the stage. I wait as I, along with others, am bestowed with my honorary PhD. I'm still waiting when President Hanlon introduces me and shows me the way to the podium.

I step up to the podium.

And then . . .

Something completely special occurs.

If you watch the video, you can see the moment it happens.

I am standing at the podium. I look out at the crowd. I take a deep breath in. I'm still waiting for it—the fear, the panic, the nerves. I'm almost asking for it. Searching for it. Looking around for it. It must be here somewhere. But when I stare out into that crowd of graduating students in their green caps and gowns, all I see is . . . me.

Twenty years ago, I sat in those chairs, in that crowd, in a green cap and gown. Just like them. I recognize them. I know them. That look on their faces. Their eyes filled with uncertainty. And I understand that the fear, the panic, the nerves I am searching for will not come for me today. It has come for them. The fear they are suffering about what lies ahead is far greater than anything I will ever be feeling. And suddenly I am okay. I am no longer afraid to talk to them. I am no longer afraid to stand there alone at the podium for twenty minutes and be honestly, vulnerably myself with them. Because once upon a time, I was them. And sometime in their futures, they will be me.

Whatever I'm going to say is not for me. It isn't for the outside world. It doesn't matter how people react to it or judge it. I'm not talking to anyone but these graduates sitting in front of me. This is just for them.

And so I exhale.

You can see it.

If you watch the video, you can see me exhale.

You can see the very last instant, the very last moment, the very last breath of my fear. From that exhale forth, I am someone new. Someone comfortable. Someone unafraid.

My body relaxes. I smile. I settle into my soul. And for the first time in my life, I stand on a stage and raise my voice to the public with full confidence and not an inch of panic. For the first time in my life, I speak to an audience as myself and I feel joy. Here is what I say:

DARTMOUTH COMMENCEMENT SPEECH

Delivered June 8, 2014

Hanover, New Hampshire

DREAMS ARE FOR LOSERS

President Hanlon, faculty, staff, honored guests, parents, students, families and friends—good morning and congratulations to the Dartmouth graduating class of 2014!

So.

This is weird.

Me giving a speech.

In general, I do not like giving speeches. Giving a speech requires standing in front of large groups of people while they look at you and it also requires talking. I can do the standing part okay. But the "you looking" and the "me talking" . . . I'm NOT a fan. I get this overwhelming feeling of fear.

Terror, really.

Dry mouth, heart beats super fast, everything gets a little bit slow motion.

Like I might pass out. Or die. Or poop my pants or something.

I mean, don't worry. I'm not going to pass out or die or poop my pants. Mainly because just by telling you it could happen, I have somehow neutralized it as an option. Like as if saying it out loud casts some kind of spell where it cannot possibly happen now.

Vomit. I could vomit.

See? Vomiting is now also off the table.

Neutralized it. We're good.

Anyway, the point is, I do not like to give speeches. I'm a writer. I'm a TV writer. I like to write stuff for other people to say. I actually contemplated bringing Ellen Pompeo or Kerry Washington here to say my speech for me . . . but my lawyer pointed out that when you drag someone across state lines against their will, the FBI comes looking for you, so . . .

So I don't like giving speeches. In general. Because of the fear. And the terror. But this speech? This speech, I really did not want to give.

A Dartmouth commencement speech?

Dry mouth. Heart beats so, so fast.

Everything in slow motion.

Pass out, die, poop.

Look, it would be fine if this were, like, twenty years ago. If it was back in the day when I graduated from Dartmouth. Twenty-three years ago, I was sitting right where you are now. And I was listening to Elizabeth Dole speak. And she was great. She was calm, she was confident. It was just . . . different. It felt like she was just talking to a group of people. Like a fireside chat with friends. Just Liddy Dole and nine thousand of her friends. Because it was twenty years ago. And she was JUST talking to a group of people.

Now? Twenty years later? This is no fireside chat. It's not just you and me. This speech is filmed and streamed and tweeted and uploaded. NPR has, like, a whole app dedicated to commencement speeches.

A WHOLE SITE JUST ABOUT COMMENCEMENT SPEECHES.

There are other sites that rate them. And mock them. And dissect them. It's weird. And stressful. And kind of vicious for an introvert perfectionist writer who hates speaking in public in the first place.

When President Hanlon called me—

By the way, I would like to thank President Hanlon for asking me way back in January, thus giving me a full six months of panic and terror to enjoy.

When President Hanlon called me, I almost said no. Almost.

Dry mouth. Heart beats so, so fast. Everything in slow motion. Pass out, die, poop.

But I'm here. I am gonna do it. I'm doing it. You know why?

Because I like a challenge. And because this year I made myself a promise to do the stuff that terrifies me. And because, twenty-plus years ago when I was trudging uphill from the River Cluster through all that snow to get to the Hop for play rehearsal, I never imagined I would one day be HERE. Standing at the Old Pine Lectern. Staring out at all of you. About to throw down on some wisdom for the Dartmouth commencement address. So, you know, moments.

Also, I'm here because I really, really wanted to eat some EBAs.

Okay.

I want to say right now that every single time someone asked me what I was going to talk about in this speech, I would boldly and confidently say that I had all kinds of wisdom to share.

I was lying.

I feel wildly unqualified to be giving advice. There is no wisdom here. So all I can do is talk about some stuff that could maybe be useful to you. From one Dartmouth grad to another. Some stuff that won't ever show up in Meredith Grey voice-overs or Papa Pope monologues. Some stuff I probably shouldn't be telling you here now. Because of the uploading and the streaming and websites. But I am going to pretend that it is twenty years ago. That it is just you and me. That we're having a fireside chat. Screw the outside world and what they think. I've already said the word *poop* like five times already anyway . . . things are getting real up in here.

Wait.

Before I talk to you, I want to talk to your parents. Because the other thing about it being twenty years later is that

I'm a mother now. So I know some things. Some very different things. I have three girls. I've been to the show. You don't know what that means. But your parents do. You think this day is all about you. But your parents . . . the people who raised you . . . the people who endured you . . . they potty-trained you, they taught you to read, they survived you as a teenager, they have suffered twenty-one years and not once did they kill you. This day . . . you call it your graduation day. But this day is not about you. This is their day. This is the day they take back their lives, this is the day they earn their freedom. This day is their independence day. Parents, I salute you. And as I have an eight-month-old, I hope to join your ranks of freedom in twenty years!!

Okay.

So here it comes. The real-deal part of my speech. Or as you may call it, *Stuff Some Random Alum Who Makes TV Shows Thinks You Should Know Before You Graduate.*

You ready? Here we go!

When people give these kinds of speeches, they usually tell you all kinds of wise and heartfelt things. They have wisdom to impart. They have lessons to share. They tell you: Follow your dreams. Listen to your spirit. Change the world. Make your mark. Find your inner voice and make it sing. Embrace failure. Dream. Dream and dream big. As a matter of fact, dream and don't stop dreaming until your dream comes true.

I think that's crap.

I think a lot of people dream. And while they are busy dreaming, the really happy people, the really successful people, the really interesting, powerful, engaged people? Are busy doing.

The dreamers. They stare at the sky and they make plans and they hope and they think and they talk about it endlessly. And they start a lot of sentences with "I want to be . . ." or "I wish . . ."

"I want to be a writer." "I wish I could travel around the world."

And they dream of it. The buttoned-up ones meet for cocktails and they all brag about their dreams. The hippie ones have vision boards and they meditate on their dreams. You write in your journal about your dreams. Or discuss it endlessly with your best friend or your girlfriend or your mother. And it feels really good. You're talking about it. You're planning it. Kind of. You are blue-skying your life. And that is what everyone says you should do. Right? That's what Oprah and Bill Gates did to get successful, right?

NO.

Dreams are lovely. But they are just dreams. Fleeting, ephemeral. Pretty. But dreams do not come true just because you dream them. It's hard work that makes things happen. It's hard work that creates change.

LESSON ONE: DITCH THE DREAM.
BE A DOER, NOT A DREAMER.

Maybe you know exactly what you dream of being. Or maybe you're paralyzed because you have no idea what your passion is. The truth is, it doesn't matter. You don't have to know. You just have to keep moving forward. You just have to keep doing something, seizing the next opportunity, staying open to trying something new. It doesn't have to fit your vision of the perfect job or the perfect life. Perfect is boring, and dreams are not real. Just . . . DO. You think, "I wish I could travel"—you sell your crappy car and buy a ticket and go to Bangkok right now. I'm serious. You say, "I want to be a writer"—guess what? A writer is someone who writes every day. Start writing. Or: You don't have a job? Get one. ANY JOB. Don't sit at home waiting for the magical dream opportunity. Who are you? Prince William? No. Get a job. Work. Do until you can do something else.

I did not dream of being a TV writer. Never, not once when I was here in the hallowed halls of the Ivy League, did I say to myself, "Self, I want to write TV."

You know what I wanted to be?

I wanted to be Nobel Prize–winning author Toni Morrison.

That was my dream. I blue-skyed it like crazy. I dreamed

and dreamed. And while I was dreaming, I was living in my sister's basement. Dreamers often end up living in the basements of relatives, FYI. Anyway, there I was in that basement; I was dreaming of being Nobel Prize–winning author Toni Morrison. Guess what? I couldn't be Nobel Prize–winning author Toni Morrison. Because Toni Morrison already had that job and she wasn't interested in giving it up. One day I was sitting in that basement and I read an article in the *New York Times* that said it was harder to get into USC film school than it was to get into Harvard Law School.

I could dream about being Toni Morrison. Or I could do.

At film school, I discovered an entirely new way of telling stories. A way that suited me. A way that brought me joy. A way that flipped this switch in my brain and changed the way I saw the world.

Years later, I had dinner with Toni Morrison.

All she wanted to talk about was *Grey's Anatomy*.

That never would have happened if I hadn't stopped dreaming of becoming her and gotten busy becoming myself.

LESSON TWO: TOMORROW IS GOING TO BE THE WORST DAY EVER FOR YOU.

When I graduated from Dartmouth that day in 1991, when I was sitting right where you are and I was staring up at Elizabeth Dole speaking, I will admit that I have no idea what she was saying. Couldn't even listen to her. Not because I was overwhelmed or emotional or any of that. But because I had a serious hangover. Like, an epic painful hangover because—

(And here is where I apologize to President Hanlon, because I know you are trying to build a better and more responsible Dartmouth and I applaud you and I admire you and it is VERY necessary . . .)

—I'd been really freaking drunk the night before. And the reason I'd been so drunk the night before, the reason I'd done upside-down margarita shots at Bones Gate, was because I knew that after graduation, I was going to take off my cap and gown, my parents were going to pack my stuff in the car and I was going to go home and probably never come back to Hanover again. And even if I did come back, it wouldn't matter because it wouldn't be the same because I didn't live here anymore.

On my graduation day, I was grieving.

My friends were celebrating. They were partying. So excited. So happy. No more school, no more books, no more teachers' dirty looks, yay. And I was like, are you freaking kidding me? You get all the fro-yo you want here! The gym is free. The apartments in Manhattan are smaller than my suite in North Mass. Who cared if there was no place to get my hair done? All my friends were here. I ran my own theater company here.

I was grieving.

I knew enough about how the world works, about how adulthood plays out, to be grieving.

Here's where I am going to embarrass myself and make you all feel better about yourselves. I literally lay on the floor of my dorm room and cried while my mother packed my room. I refused to help her. Like, refused. Like, hell no I won't go. I nonviolent-protested leaving here. Like, went limp like a protester only without the chanting—it was really pathetic.

Don't you feel better?

If none of you lie facedown on a dirty hardwood floor and cry today while your mommy packs up your dorm room, you are already starting your careers out ahead of me. You are winning.

But here's the thing. The thing I really felt like I knew. The real world sucks. And it is scary.

College is awesome.

You're special here. You're in the Ivy League, you are at the pinnacle of your life's goals at this point—your entire life up until now has been about getting into a great college and then graduating from that college. And now, today, you have done it. Yay!

The moment you get out of college, you think you are going to take the world by storm. All doors will be opened to you. It's going to be laughter and diamonds and soirees left and right.

What really happens is that, to the rest of the world, you are now the bottom of the heap. Maybe an intern. Possibly a low-paid assistant. At best. And it is awful. The real world, it sucked so badly for me. I felt like a loser all the time. And more than a loser? I felt lost.

Which brings me to clarify LESSON NUMBER TWO: *Tomorrow IS going to be the worst day ever for you.*

But don't be an asshole.

Here's the thing. Yes, it is hard out there. But hard? Is relative. I come from a middle-class family, my parents are academics, I was born after the civil rights movement, I was a toddler during the women's movement, I live in the United States of America, all of which means I'm allowed to own my freedom, my rights, my voice and my uterus and I went to Dartmouth and earned an Ivy League degree.

The lint in my navel that accumulated while I gazed at it as I suffered from feeling lost about how hard it was to not feel special after graduation . . . that navel lint was embarrassed for me.

Elsewhere in the world, girls are being harmed simply because they want to get an education. Slavery still exists. Children still die from malnutrition. In this country, we lose more people to handgun violence than any other nation in the world. Sexual assault against women in America is pervasive and disturbing and continues at an alarming rate.

So yes, tomorrow may suck for you—as it did for me. But as you stare at the lint in your navel, have some perspective.

We are incredibly lucky. We have been given a gift. An incredible education has been placed before us. We ate all the fro-yo we could get our hands on. We skied. We had EBAs at one a.m. We built bonfires and got frostbite and enjoyed all the free treadmills. We beer-ponged our asses off.

Now it's time to pay it forward.

Find a cause you love. It's okay to just pick one. You are going to need to spend a lot of time out in the real world trying to figure out how to stop being a lost loser so one cause is good. But find *one*. And devote some time every week to it.

And while we are discussing this, let me say a thing. A hashtag is not helping.

#yesallwomen

#takebackthenight

#notallmen

#bringbackourgirls

#StopPretendingHashtagsAreTheSameAsDoingSomething

Hashtags are very pretty on Twitter. I love them. I will hashtag myself into next week. But a hashtag is not a movement. A hashtag does not make you Dr. King. A hashtag does not change anything. It's a hashtag. It's you, sitting on your butt, typing into your computer and then going back to binge-watching your favorite show. For me, it's *Game of Thrones*.

Volunteer some hours. Focus on something outside your-self. Devote a slice of your energies toward making the world suck less every week. Some people suggest that doing this will increase your sense of well-being. Some say it's just good karma. I say that it will allow you to remember that, whether you are a legacy or the first in your family to go to college, the air you are breathing right now is rare air. Appreciate it. And don't be an asshole.

LESSON THREE

So you're giving back and you're out there doing and it's working. Life is good. You are making it. You're a success. And it's exciting and great. At least it is for me. I love my life. I have three TV shows at work and I have three daughters at home. And it's all amazing. I am truly happy.

And people are constantly asking me, how do you do it?

And usually, they have this sort of admiring and amazed tone.

Shonda, how do you do it all?

Like I'm full of magical magic and wisdom and special-ness.

How do you do it all?

And I usually just smile and say, "I'm really organized." Or if I'm feeling slightly kind, I say, "I have a lot of help."

And those things are true. But they also aren't true.

And this is the thing that I really want to say. To all of you. Not just to the women out there. Although this will matter to you women a great deal as you enter the workforce and try to figure out how to juggle work and family. But it will also matter to the men. Who I think increasingly are also trying to figure out how to juggle work and family. And frankly, if you are not trying to figure it out, men of Dartmouth? You should be. Fatherhood is being redefined at a lightning-fast rate. You don't want to be a dinosaur.

So women AND men of Dartmouth: as you try to figure out the impossible task of juggling work and family and you hear over and over and over again that you just need a lot of help or you just need to be organized or you just need to try just a little bit harder . . . as a very successful woman, a single mother of three, who constantly gets asked the question "How do you do it all?" For once I am going to answer that question with 100 percent honesty here for you now.

Because it's just us.

Because it's our fireside chat.

Because somebody has to tell you the truth.

Shonda, how do you do it all?

The answer is this: I don't.

Whenever you see me somewhere succeeding in one area of my life, that almost certainly means that I am failing in another area of my life.

If I am killing it on a *Scandal* script for work, I'm probably missing bath and story time at home. If I am at home sewing my kids' Halloween costumes, I am probably blowing off a script I was supposed to rewrite. If I'm accepting a prestigious award, I'm missing my baby's first swim lesson. If I am at my daughter's debut in her school musical, I am missing Sandra Oh's last scene ever being filmed at *Grey's Anatomy*.

If I am succeeding at one, I am inevitably failing at the other.

That is the trade-off.

That is the Faustian bargain one makes with the devil that comes with being a powerful working woman who is also a powerful mother. You never feel 100 percent okay, you never get your sea legs, you are always a little nauseous.

Something is always lost.

Something is always missing.

And yet.

I want my daughters to see me and know me as a woman who works. I want that example set for them. I like how proud they are when they come to my offices and know that they come to Shondaland.

There is a land and it is named after their mother.

In their world, mothers run companies. In their world, mothers own Thursday nights. In their world, mothers work. And I am a better mother for it. The woman I am because I get to run Shondaland, because I get to write all day, because I get to spend my days making things up, that woman is a better person—and a better mother. Because that woman is happy. That woman is fulfilled. That woman is whole. I wouldn't want them to know the me that didn't get to do this all day long. I wouldn't want them to know the me who wasn't doing.

SO.

Lesson NUMBER THREE is that ANYONE WHO TELLS YOU THEY ARE DOING IT ALL PERFECTLY IS A LIAR.

Okay.

I fear that I have scared you. Or that I have been bleak. That was not my intention. It is my hope that you run out of here excited, leaning forward, into the wind, ready to take the world by storm. That would be so very fabulous. For you to do what everyone expects of you. For you to just go be exactly the picture of hard-core Dartmouth awesome.

My point, I think, is that it is okay if you don't. My point is that it can be scary to graduate. That you can lie on the hard-wood floor of your dorm room and cry while your mom packs up your stuff. That you can have an impossible dream to be Toni Morrison that you have to let go of. That every day you can feel like you might be failing at work or at your home life. That the real world is hard.

And yet.

You can still wake up every single morning and go, "I have three amazing kids and I have created work that I am proud of and I absolutely love my life and I would not trade it for anyone else's life ever."

You can still wake up one day and find yourself living a life you never even imagined dreaming of.

My dreams did not come true. But I worked really hard. And I ended up building an empire out of my imagination. So my dreams? Can suck it.

You can wake up one day and find that you are interesting and powerful and engaged. You can wake up one day and find that you are a doer.

You can be sitting right where you are now. Looking up at me. Probably—hopefully, I pray for you—hungover. And then twenty years from now, you can wake up and find yourself in the Hanover Inn full of fear and terror because you are going to give the commencement speech.

Dry mouth.

Heart beats so, so fast.

Everything in slow motion.

Pass out, die, poop.

Which one of you will it be? Which member of the class of 2014 will find themselves standing here at the Old Pine Lectern? I checked and it is pretty rare for an alum to speak here. It's pretty much me and Robert Frost and Mr. Rogers.

Which is CRAZY AWESOME.

Which one of you is going to make it up here? I hope it is you. Yes. You. Seriously. You.

No. Seriously. You.

When it happens, you'll know what it feels like.

Dry mouth.

Heart beats so, so fast.

Everything in slow motion.

Graduates, every single one of you, be proud of your accomplishments. Make good on your diplomas.

Remember, you are no longer students. You are no longer works in progress. You are now citizens of the real world. You have a responsibility to become a person worthy of joining and contributing to society.

Who you are today . . . that's who you are.

Be brave.

Be amazing.

Be worthy.

And every single time you get the chance?

Stand up in front of people.

Let them see you. Speak. Be heard.

Go ahead and have the dry mouth.

Let your heart beat so, so fast.

Watch everything move in slow motion.

So what. You what?

You pass out, you die, you poop?

No.

(And this is really the only lesson you'll ever need to know.)

You take it in.
You breathe this rare air.
You feel alive.
You are yourself.
You are truly finally always yourself.
Thank you. Good luck.

6

Yes to Surrendering the Mommy War (Or, Jenny McCarthy Is My Everything)

I have an amazing nanny.

She's wonderful and soulful. She has a sly sense of humor—I've seen her deliver a funnier joke with a single silent raise of her eyebrow than many stand-up comedians. She guards a very sensitive heart—any human suffering brings her to tears. She's smart. Talk down to her and find yourself mentally slapped. She's an excellent judge of character and seems to know an original spirit from a forgery every time. Cross boundaries with her or her charges in any improper way and suffer the wrath of a lion. Get down on your hands and knees with her and the kids, and she will patiently teach and teach until something in you cracks open and you remember who you were as a child and begin to play.

She's principled and firm, rude behavior doesn't materialize in her presence. She's a grown-up who fully sees and knows children as citizens and people and souls. And because she respects children, all children seem to respect her. She is a goddess sent by the universe through the grace of the stars.

Her name is Jenny.

Jenny McCarthy.

I'm not kidding.

She has the same name as a well-known TV personality. A TV personality whose ideas about vaccinations my Jenny McCarthy does not happen to share, she'd want me to tell you.

Jenny McCarthy says vaccinate your kids.

I hired Jenny McCarthy fifteen minutes after I met her. At least, I tried to. She resisted. She had questions. She interviewed *me*. I was nervous. I knew immediately that Jenny McCarthy was a person I wanted in my house, with my family, around my children. I wanted to know her and I wanted to have her know us. As Olivia Pope would say, trust your gut. I trusted my gut. I knew Jenny McCarthy was for us. She has a good heart.

Once, in trying to describe her to someone, I referred to her as a new-wave Mary Poppins, but really, that's not true. She's way more awesome than that Poppins chick. Have you watched that movie as an adult? I mean, really butt-in-the-seat, stare-at-the-screen watched that movie as an adult? Because, if you ask me, Mary Poppins was not a very good nanny. All she had was a bag of endless objects and a kick-ass umbrella. Also I'm pretty sure she was doing drugs and having sex with that chimney sweep.

About two weeks after Jenny began working at the house, she looked at me thoughtfully and said, "You know, I'm your nanny too. Because, Shonda, you need a nanny."

I think maybe I should have been insulted. I mean, she *did* just call me a child. Right? I should have felt some outrage or some affront. Instead, what I felt, overwhelmingly, was relief.

I had been out battling on the front line, doing the best I could against the enemy. But I was battered and bruised. Bombs kept dropping everywhere, I was tiptoeing around land mines left and right. I wanted to go home. I was losing the Mommy War something terrible.

I don't know about you, but the mistakes and missteps I have made since becoming a mother . . . before kids, my confidence could not be dented. Now it's shattered on a daily basis. *I don't know what I am doing.* There is no manual. There's no checklist. There was no one to give lessons. These tiny humans have me caught up, trapped me behind enemy lines. I willingly enlisted, but did I do it for the right reasons? I worry that all I wanted was to look cute in the uniform. Or maybe be in the USO—sing for the troops. Well, I can't sing. But I can play the oboe. Give me a chance and I will play the *hell* out of an oboe for the troops. Instead I am fighting. Front lines. Holding a weapon. I'm not as brave as the others. Not as smart or as strong or as sure that I can make it.

You know the character in the old war movies who always gets shot because he panics and runs?

That character is me as a mother.

I needed help. I needed fresh troops. Or more ammo. Or a medic. Or even just a chaplain for last rites, for the love of . . .

I got Jenny McCarthy.

Jenny McCarthy is the SEAL Team Six of nannies.

I cannot count the number of times some nice reporter has placed a little battered silver recorder in front of my face, flicked it on and, with a kind smile, asked me what I call the Big Questions: *How do I manage work and home? What tips do I have for working moms? What is my secret to finding balance in a busy world?*

I get asked the Big Questions in almost EVERY SINGLE INTERVIEW I do. I hate the Big Questions. I hate being asked the Big Questions ALMOST as much as I hate being asked the Diversity Question—"Why is diversity so important?" (which ranks for me as one of the dumbest questions on the face of the earth, right up there with "Why do people need food and air?" and "Why should women be feminists?").

But as much as I hate the Big Questions, I don't want to be rude to the very nice reporters who ask. I don't think the reporters mean any harm in posing the questions—I think people genuinely wonder. It's just that, before this Year of

Yes, I genuinely didn't know what to say. So I'd find myself smiling at the reporters and giving a lot of different, odd answers.

"Why, Jane, I manage with a lot of organization and a label maker."

"I do laundry *late at night*, Susan."

"Gosh dangit, Bill, I've started meditating on a regular basis!"

Yeah, right. *Late-night laundry* is the cure to getting three kids up and dressed, working a twelve-hour day, making calls to my kid's tutor, scheduling doctor's appointments and play-dates on my only ten-minute break and then coming home to find that my one-year-old finally walked and *I missed it*?

Late-night laundry, my ass.

Late-night laundry is not a true answer to any question ever.

There is one answer to all of those reporters' Big Questions.

I just didn't want to say it.

Because no one else ever said it.

I've read a lot of books written by and about working women and I'm struck by the fact no one ever seems to want to talk about having help at home. Which I think is not so helpful to the women who *don't* have help at home.

Let me put this in completely irrelevant and strange hair-related terms:

God bless the soul of Whitney Houston, but I spent an hour every single morning of all four years of high school in front of the mirror trying to get my hair to look exactly like Whitney's hair. Hours and hours of my life given over to a hot curling iron and a bottle of hair spray and burned fingertips. To me, Whitney's hair was the definition of flawless. As a teenager in Coke-bottle-thick glasses who barely spoke at school and spent all her time inside books, nothing about my life was flawless. I somehow believed that everything would be better if I could just make my hair look like Whitney's. If my hair was flawless, my life would follow suit. Because clearly Whitney had it all worked out.

I was at a hair salon in Los Angeles five or six years after graduating from college. For some reason, Whitney came up in the usual hair salon gossip. I casually mentioned to my hairdresser how much I'd loved her hairstyle when I was in high school and then spun the story of my morning Whitney ritual. I made sure that I danced around the sad determination and kept the story funny. Gotta lay that track, gotta burn that campfire. So my hairdresser was still wiping the tears of laughter from her face when she said it.

"Girl"—she shook her head—"you know that was a wig she had on, right? You could probably buy it if you want to. Hold on. Let me get the wig catalogue and show you . . ."

I did not hear another word she said. I was lost, thinking of the hours of wasted time and the gallons of wasted hair spray. I relived the inevitable misery, the feeling of failure and insecurity that came every morning when my hair wouldn't do what I was trying to bully it into doing.

And if I had known . . . if I had just been told . . . no matter how hard I worked, my hair was NEVER going to look like that . . .

If I had only known that not even *Whitney's* hair could look like that . . .

I had to bite my lip hard to keep from bursting into tears right then and there in front of two ladies I didn't know.

Black hair salons are no joke—I was going to be sitting across from these two ladies for at least five more hours. I did not want to be known as the Fool Who Sobbed While She Got Her Hair Relaxed.

I didn't cry. But it hurt. The betrayal ran deep.

But, I have to admit, there was also a small sense of relief.

Because now I knew: I had not failed.

I just didn't *own the wig*.

Successful, powerful working mothers who keep silent about how they take care of their homes and families, who behave as if they maybe have a clone of themselves or possess Hermione Granger's Time-Turner so they can be two places at once . . . well, they are making everyone else get out their curling irons.

Don't do that. Don't make me get my curling iron out for no reason.

Jenny McCarthy is my family's nanny. And I am proud to say so out loud to anyone who asks. I am proud to say that I do not do this alone.

I don't think powerful, famous women hide the fact that they have nannies or some kind of help at home because they are being unkind to other people. I mean, these women aren't at home laughing and laughing at how everyone out in America is trying to do it all and can't because they don't know that the secret is that NO ONE CAN DO IT ALL! HA HA!! We fooled you! SUCKA!

I don't even think that's why my idol didn't tell us she wore the wig.

Powerful famous women don't say out loud that they have help at home, that they have nannies, housekeepers, chefs, assistants, stylists—whatever it is they have to keep their worlds spinning—they don't say out loud that they have these people at home doing these jobs because they are ashamed.

Or maybe a more precise way to say it is that these women have *been shamed*.

Before my daughter Harper was born, when I was still filling out stacks and stacks of adoption paperwork, smiling for social workers and obsessing over baby clothes in stores— back when having a baby was more one of my brilliant ideas than anything else—a working friend asked me if I had started interviewing.

"Interviewing for what?" I remember asking her.

"You know. A baby nurse, a nanny." She had a new baby herself, a little boy less than six months old. I can still picture her as she said this. She leaned forward in her chair, more intense than I thought the discussion merited. As if she was trying to tell me something important. And of course she was. She *so* was.

She was wasting her time.

I am never more sure of myself about a topic than when I have absolutely no experience with it. So with no baby of my own anywhere in sight, I was incredibly sure of myself as a mother.

If I could slap myself, just reach back in time and wallop a good one across my face . . .

Because what I did next . . .

Look, it didn't feel like much at the time. In my defense, I wasn't yet a mother. I didn't yet know. I'm innocent!

Ignorance is no excuse.

What I did next was cruel. And from where I stand now, after thirteen years fighting deep behind the enemy lines of the Mother Hood, I can tell you with certainty: any tribunal would call it a war crime. What I did next was launch a violent emotional ambush that left my unarmed sister wounded in the field.

I looked at my friend. She had dark circles of exhaustion under her eyes. I'm pretty sure her hair hadn't been washed in weeks. She'd blown her nose with baby wipes earlier. I took all of this in. And I said:

"Why in the world would I *hire* someone to take care of my baby? I mean, seriously? That's just lazy. If I'm not willing to take care of my baby myself, why am I even *having* a baby in the first place?"

I felt all the mighty righteousness in the world.

Her face tightened. The air between us changed. I felt startled by her rage.

Mom down, mom down.

I can't tell you exactly how that meal ended, what was said. But I can tell you that she did not speak to me again.

Ever.

It wasn't until later that I got it. I had an eight-week-old Harper strapped to my chest in a Snugli. I was sweaty; my hair, which had been a cute Afro puff a week or so ago, was now not merely dirty—it was a matted, terrifying Afro-mess that was going to be both painful and time-consuming to try to restore. The pajamas I wore had a stiff, hard patch of dried formula on the front. That stiff, hard patch acted as a fine bug repellant, because it stank like nothing I'd ever smelled before. I was seated in front of my computer, alternately sobbing from an exhaustion so total that I felt sure I could SEE the air moving in blue waves around the room, and trying to write dialogue for the movie I was supposed to have turned in a month ago.

That was how stupid I was. I adopted a baby and still agreed to turn in a script for a movie a *month* later.

If you have no children, trust me: THAT IS BEYOND STUPID.

Later that evening, Christopher arrived. This is Chris #2 for those of you keeping score—not my publicist, Chris. This Chris and I used to be roommates a hundred years ago when we were both broke and struggling. Now he's a lawyer with a wife and an adorable son. I was best man at his wedding. He is Harper's godfather, and he takes that job very seriously. Every Sunday for the past twelve years, he has showed up at my door to spend time with his godchild. Every. Single. Sunday. He got married on a Saturday, and the next day he was at my house. I told him to go home. He told me it was Sunday in a tone that allowed no argument. He's not just a friend—he's family.

So when Chris #2 arrived that evening, he took one look at me and removed the baby from my arms. He gave me that smile you give a person who has the crazy, swirly eyes. He also took a big step back at the smell of me.

"Go take a shower. Harper and I are going to watch ESPN."

When I woke up an hour later I was still in the shower, the now cold water causing me to shiver. I thought: "I need help. I need to hire some help. I need to hire a lot of help. Or I am going to lose my job and my child and I are going to starve to death. I need to hire help or I won't make it."

And I suddenly thought of my friend.

I thought of what I had said to her.

Mom down, mom down.

I thought of what I had done to her.

I'd shamed her.

We've all been taught to shame and be ashamed. And why wouldn't we feel ashamed? How could we not feel ashamed?

We're not supposed to have any help. We're supposed to do it all ourselves. Even if we are working. So if you have kids and you get help to care for them?

SHAME ON YOU.

Which is just . . . rude.

And sexist.

Caterina Scorsone (who also happens to play Amelia Shepherd on *Grey's Anatomy* and *Private Practice*) and I spend a lot of time ranting to each other about this issue.

"No man," she points out often, "has *ever* had to apologize for having help in order to take care of his home and his kids. *Ever.* Why do we?"

She has a point. *Why do we?*

I mean, let's all remember that for *most* women, staying home is not an option. Most women have to work. The majority of women, unless they are wealthy or financially cared for by someone else, have to work. Historically, women have always had to work. Women worked in the fields. Women were maids. Women raised other women's children. Women were nurses. Women worked in factories. Women were secretaries. Seamstresses. Telephone operators.

What was different in the past was that people lived closer to their families. Your mother watched your children. Your aunt watched them. Your sister. Your cousin Sue. For some people, this remains true. For most people . . . you need help. And the crisis of child care in this country is brutal. And scary. And expensive. It's a lot to handle. I'm betting you are having a hard time doing it all, feeling good about it and making it all work.

So it would not help anyone to pick up this book and read that I merrily tuck a giggling toddler under each arm with effortless ease and skip to my office, where I run two shows and produce two more while developing others as I laugh and laugh and sip champagne with celebrities while we all eat mounds of food and never gain a pound . . .

It never *ever* helps to think that Whitney's hairdo is *real*.

Leave no mom behind, soldiers. And even *with* help . . . I'm still in the trenches. Nobody has this thing figured out.

Except doesn't it *feel* like everyone else has figured it out?

I don't know about you, but it's the idea that I'm not measuring up that gets me. I'm constantly worrying and wondering and feeling like I am failing because everywhere I look, everyone else seems to be thriving. The women around me are smiling and their kids are smiling and their houses

seem clean and it all looks so great on Pinterest and Instagram and Facebook . . .

I am not an "everything looks great" mom. I am a "barely
hanging on" mom.

I am a hot-mess mama.

I have worn pajamas in the carpool line.

Dirty pajamas.

A long long looooong time ago, at one of the schools my
daughter thankfully no longer attends, I was sitting in that
back-to-school meeting that all schools have at the end of
summer. After the principal gave a warm and rousing welcome, she invited the head of the PTA to the stage. Now, the
head of the PTA was a school parent. A mom. A mom just like
any other mom. If any other mom was tall, gorgeous, whip-
smart and—I gotta say it—practically perfect in every way.

Perfect PTA Mom very cheerfully began to tell us about
the rules for the Friday bake sale rotation schedule that we
were all expected to take part in. (Now, why we were filling
our kids up with sugary baked goods and why we were *selling*
them these baked goods in an effort to raise money when the
tuition at this school already made me involuntarily shudder
every time I thought about it . . . was all beyond me. But
there was a weekly bake sale and we all had to join in. For
Perfect PTA Mom told us so.)

"Finally," this PTA mom finished up, "just so we don't
have any problems like last year, I just want to be clear: all of

the baked goods must be homemade, something you make with your child. That's so much nicer."

Now, maybe it's the Midwesterner in me.

Or the common sense in me.

Or the hot-mess mama in me.

It was something.

Before I even knew it was happening, my mouth had opened and I was speaking in a voice that carried loud and clear across the auditorium.

"Are you *fucking* kidding me?!"

Really loud. LOUD. LOOOOUUD.

Heads whipped around in my direction. Try being *that* mom at your kid's school. I didn't even know I had that in me. But I did. I was mad. I was insulted.

I have a time-consuming job. A job that I love. A job that I love and that I wouldn't trade for the world. But being a writer invades my brain twenty-four hours a day. I dream about the shows. The job takes from me in ways I never expected. And yet I am devoted to it. To the rush, to the track laying, to the *work*.

I *work*. I have a job.

People with jobs often do not have time to bake.

"But being a mother is *also* a job, Shonda."

I can hear someone reading this book saying those words right now.

You know what I say to that?

NO.

IT IS NOT.

Being a mother is not a job.

Stop throwing things at me.

I'm sorry but it is not.

I find it offensive to motherhood to call being a mother a job.

Being a mother *isn't* a job.

It's who someone is.

It's who I am.

You can quit a job. I can't quit being a mother. I'm a mother forever. Mothers are never off the clock, mothers are never on vacation. Being a mother redefines us, reinvents us, destroys and rebuilds us. Being a mother brings us face-to-face with ourselves as children, with our mothers as human beings, with our darkest fears of who we really are. Being a mother requires us to get it together or risk messing up another person forever. Being a mother yanks our hearts out of our bodies and attaches them to our tiny humans and sends them out into the world, forever hostages.

If all of that happened at work, I'd have quit fifty times already. Because there isn't enough money in the world. And my job does not pay me in the smell of baby head and the soft weight of snuggly sleepy toddler on my shoulder. Being a mother is incredibly important. To the naysayers, I growl, do not *diminish* it by calling it a job.

And please, don't ever try to tell me it's the most important job I'll ever have as a way of trying to convince me to stay at home with my children all day.

Don't.

I might punch you in the nose.

The most important job to a woman who has rent, has a car note, has utility bills and needs groceries is one that pays her money to keep her family alive.

Let's stop trying to make ourselves indulge in the crappy mythological lady-cult that makes being a mother seem like work.

Staying at home with your children is an incredible choice to make. And it's awesome and admirable if you make it. Go you.

Being a mother still happens if you don't stay home with your kids. It still happens if you get a job and go to work. It happens if you are an Army Ranger and you're deployed overseas and your kid is staying with your parents.

Still a mother.

Still not a job.

Working or staying home, one is still a mother.

One is not better than the other. Both choices are worthy of the same amount of respect.

Motherhood remains equally, painfully death defying and difficult either way.

It does, it does.

Let's all put down our weapons for a minute, okay?

Perhaps you think that it is important to your child's personal growth to bake goods in your house. More power to you, my sister. I will defend your right to bake your brownies, I will march for your right to home-bake whatever you damn well want to home-bake. But I will take off my earrings and ask someone to hold my purse for the verbal beatdown we will need to engage in if you try to tell me that I must define *my motherhood* in the same terms as yours.

There's room enough for everybody here.

This is a big, big maternity tent.

If I want to buy my brownies from Costco and drop them off in a wrinkled brown paper bag still wrapped in the plastic and foil container with the orange price sticker still attached, guess what?

That's how it's gonna go down.

Suck it, judgies.

I am not telling you to do it that way. You go bake your *ass* off. But we all have to acknowledge that our way is not *the* way.

Did I judge your perfectly made, piping-hot, double-fudge chocolate cupcakes with the hand-whipped frosting? Did I judge the beautiful monogrammed cupcake holder with the coordinating starched apron you have on?

No, I did not.

Because you are my sister.

Also, because I am going to eat all of your cupcakes.

Look, I am devoted to my children. Deeply. But my devotion has nothing to do with home-baked goods. It has nothing to do with making any kind of public show of maternal fabulousness. Because—you know me by now—public displays of any kind of fabulousness are never going to happen for me. I am devoted to knowing my children, to reading books with them, to hearing the stories they tell me and to the conversations we have. To making them citizens of the world. To raising strong feminist human beings who love and believe in themselves. That is hard enough for me without delivering home-baked goods to school on a Friday.

I'm never going to braid anyone's pigtails perfectly. No one's clothes are ever going to be ironed. Clean, yes. Ironed? Not by me. We will never make special crafts for every holiday and then take photos of them to put on Pinterest and Facebook.

Ever.

Never ever.

I will always be resentful of mom activities that take place on a Tuesday at eleven a.m. As if the mothers with jobs are not valued or welcome.

And I am always going to yell "What the fuck!" at the PTA meeting if you tell me the brownies need to be homemade.

I am already in the middle of a Great Mommy War and

it is against my worst enemy—me. I don't need another war against you. I'm betting you don't need one either.

Stacy McKee (who is one of the new head writers at *Grey's Anatomy* but started out way back in the beginning as the assistant on the show) IS the kind of mom who does crafts with her kids and puts photos of them up on Pinterest and Instagram. She works long, hard hours but still, you go into her office and as she's talking scripts and story, she's hot-gluing beads onto a princess cape for her daughter. I always furrow my brow and ask her why the hell she is doing this. Why? Or why the hell is she delicately hand-painting vistas onto Easter eggs? Or why is she doing any number of crazy amazing crafty things Stacy does for her kids? For the love of wine, why?

Stacy will furrow her brow back at me, equally confused. "Why wouldn't I?" she says.

See, Stacy LOVES doing this stuff. She'd probably do it even if she didn't have kids. Oh wait. I knew her back when she didn't have kids and she WAS doing it. Stacy once spent days making incredibly lifelike renderings of all the *Grey's Anatomy* characters out of pipe cleaners.

PIPE CLEANERS.

So it's not about working moms vs. nonworking moms. It's about people who love hot-gluing beads on capes vs. people who do not know what a hot-glue gun *is*.

And it's not even that.

It's about the non–glue gun people not assuming the glue gun people are judging them, and vice versa. Maybe don't start out with your weapons raised. Maybe that Perfect PTA Mom didn't even realize that homemade brownies could be a hardship. Maybe instead of yelling obscenities at the mention of homemade brownies, it would be better to stand up and gently point out that not everyone has the time or the bandwidth to make brownies.

And if you are met with condescension, *then* yell the obscenities.

This year, at Emerson's new preschool, I was in charge of the cake for the end–of–the–year party. I got lucky and found a bakery that can reproduce photos on a cake. I don't know how they do it and I don't care. I ordered from the bakery and showed up at the party with my awesome store-bought cake. Every child's face smiling out of the frosting. Everyone oohed and aahed. I felt victorious. In a sick, competitive, not–allowed–to–play–Scrabble, kicked–off–of–team–sports maternal fabulousness kind of way. And then someone asked me where the cake cutter was.

I brought the cake.

I did not bring anything with which to cut the cake. Or plates on which to eat the cake. Or any utensils.

At the other school, this might have been an international incident for me. Things might have escalated to nuclear levels. Arsenals would have been emptied.

But now, at this school?

I said, "Um, the cake is sooo pretty."

And I got a laugh. A friendly laugh.

Then someone grinned and said, "No big deal. I have some cake-cutting stuff!"

And everyone just moved on. Cake was served. Cake was consumed. Everyone copied down the name of the bakery off the side of the box. That was that.

These moms leave no mom behind.

I love it here.

I don't think they are different from the moms at the other school. It is that I am different. All the moms were great all along. I just couldn't see it. Now, I'm no longer looking for the enemy. So I no longer see the enemy.

And so finally, in this year, I allow myself to fully lay down my weapons.

When a reporter flicks on that recorder, smiles and asks the Big Questions, I do not call in the troops. I do not raise my shields.

I allow myself to be seen.

"How do you manage work and home? What tips do you have for working moms? What *is* your secret to finding balance in a busy world?"

Yes, I can answer now.

No hot-glue gun.

No home-baked goods.

No late-night laundry.

Leave no mom behind.

"Jenny McCarthy. To do it all, I have Jenny McCarthy."

I feel really good.

Of course, the reporter walks away deeply confused as to why Jenny McCarthy seems to figure so prominently in my life.

But I don't care.

I wave the white flag.

There is victory in surrender.

Curling irons down, my sisters.

The Mommy War has ended.

7

Yes to All Play and No Work

As the Year of Yes began to really go forward, something happened.

I got busier.

And busier.

And busier.

The more I said yes to things that challenged me, the more I had to leave the house. Saying yes had turned little cocooned me into a big social butterfly.

I flew to New York to see Kerry Washington guest-host *Saturday Night Live.* I went to the private parties of incredibly interesting people. I threw a fund-raiser for the Democratic National Committee. I helped host charity events. There were a lot of awards that year because now there was not only one show starring a black woman on Thursday night—there were two. And all three shows on Thursday were from Shondaland. My publicist, Chris, was smartly taking advantage of the fact that I was saying yes and booking as many interviews as he could squeeze into my schedule. I did my first *Good Morning America* interview with Robin Roberts. I went with the cast of *Scandal* to *The View*. I was photographed by Annie Leibovitz. I did a live interview in front of an audience at the Smithsonian. I felt like I was everywhere.

And I was. Everywhere, it seemed, but at home.

Which makes sense. All the things that would challenge me happened outside my home. Inside my home? Doing just fine.

At least I thought I was.

I mean, I was still a hot-mess mama. I was still working too much. I still needed Jenny McCarthy to nanny both the kids and me. I still needed help. I still wasn't getting enough sleep.

But I really thought I was doing fine.

Except I started to feel . . . irrelevant.

In my own home.

I'd come home and Emerson and Beckett would glance my way, give me a nod and then continue playing. Like I was the nice neighbor lady visiting from next door. Or Harper would eye me with disdain when I asked her which friend she was talking about and I'd realize I had missed a whole week's worth of discussions—a lifetime in tween years.

And then I hit an emotional wall.

One night I was all dressed up in a ball gown, hair and makeup done perfectly, borrowed diamonds shimmering on my neck and wrists. Ready to head out to some event that I had said *yes* to. And as I walked through the foyer to the front door, my daughter Emerson came rushing toward me.

"MAMA!!" she was hollering, sticky hands outstretched. "Wanna play?"

For a split second, it felt like time froze. Like in one of those action movies where everything goes into slow motion, then spins around—just before the hero dude (because somehow in the time-freezing, slow-mo, spin-around movies it is ALWAYS a dude) kicks someone's ass. But there's Emerson, her one curly tuft of hair bound into a valiant attempt at a ponytail on the top of her head in a way that makes her look like Tweety Bird. She's frozen, then moving toward me in slow motion, and then the whole room is spinning around and I can see myself: the blue ball gown, the sticky hands, the child hurtling through space toward me.

She's asked me a question.

"Wanna play?"

I'm late. I'm perfectly, elegantly dressed. Carolina Herrera made this gown. The shoes I'm wearing are some kind of navy lace that I find extremely painful, but damn, they look good on me. When I step out onto the stage, the speech I've written for this particular evening in tribute to a friend is funny and vibrant and moving. I know it will be a special moment, something the town will probably talk about the next day. My phone keeps buzzing repeatedly. It's Chris, my publicist. I really should be arriving just about now. But . . .

"Wanna play?"

There's that round face. Big hopeful eyes. She's got cupid-red lips.

I could bend down, grab her hands in mine before she touches me. Give her a soft kiss and tell her, "No. No, Mama has to go, Mama can't be late."

I could.

I'd be well within my rights. It wouldn't be unheard-of. It would be okay. She'd understand.

But in this frozen moment, I'm realizing something.

She didn't call me "*Honey*."

She's not calling everyone "*Honey*" anymore.

She's changing. Right before my eyes. The baby who was on my hip that last Thanksgiving is going to be three years old on her next birthday.

I'm missing it.

And if I'm not careful, she's going to see the back of my head heading out the door more than she'll see my face.

So in that split second, everything changes.

I kick off my painful high heels. I drop to my knees on the hardwood floor, making the ball gown pouf up around my waist like some kind of navy confection. It's going to wrinkle. I don't care.

"Wanna play?" she's asked.

"YES," I say. "Yes, I do."

And I grab those sticky hands in mine and Emerson plops herself down into my lap, laughing as the gown flies up around her.

When I arrive at the venue, fifteen minutes late, the navy ball gown is hopelessly wrinkled and I'm carrying my heels in my hand. But I don't care—there's a hot pearl of joy in my chest that is warming me in a way I'd forgotten was possible. That little fire inside of me has been reignited. Like magic.

Let's not get carried away.

It's just love. That's all it is.

We played. Emerson and I. And we were joined by Beckett and then later Harper. There was a lot of laughing. I gave my best reading of the finest book ever written—*Everyone Poops*. There may have been some dancing and singing to a made-up funky disco version of "Head, Shoulders, Knees and Toes."

There were sticky kisses. Beckett jammed her finger into my nose out of curiosity. Emerson put her head against my chest and listened until she heard my heart. Then she looked at me solemnly. "You are still alive."

Yes, I am.

Days like this, I am still alive.

We finished with our daily performance of that damned gorgeous song Idina Menzel sings in *Frozen* that has some sort of Pied Piper magical hold on all children. Then I got in the car to go to the event. Happy. That warm joy in me. Feeling fundamentally changed. Like I knew a secret that very few people get to learn.

But really, it was just love. That's no secret.

It's just something we forget.

We could all use a little more love.

A lot more love.

I am not a naturally optimistic person. I'm too in my own head to be a constant source of cheer. I have to work at happy. Dark and twisty is where my brain likes to settle. So I can use some reminders of what is good and optimistic and glass-half-full about this world. And nothing does that for me like the faces and souls of my tiny humans.

yesyesyesyesyesyesyesyesyesyesyesyesyesyesyesyes

That night, I come home and engage in what I call the Hollywood Single Mom part of my evening, which involves my forcing the nearest awake human over four feet tall to free me from whatever dress and undergarment contraptions my glam team trapped me in hours before. There have been times in New York where the task has fallen upon a very nice hotel maid. A couple of times, actors from my shows have saved me. Once in Martha's Vineyard, I was forced to ask the very proper older gentleman who was my driver for the afternoon.

(Are you judging? I see that look on your face. Uh-uh.

What did I say at the beginning of this book? Well, you are definitely *not* gonna come up here all the way in the middle of this book and judge me. It was either ask or spend the entire night sleeping in a white cocktail dress.)

This time, thankfully, I can ask my babysitter. There's a corset involved, and as soon as there's air flowing back into all parts of my lungs, I pull on a robe and go stick my face around doorways to peek at my sleeping kids.

Staring at each of my girls, I make a decision.

Whenever Emerson or Beckett or Harper (in her own way) asks, "Wanna play?"

I am always going to answer: *YES*.

Always.

Because if I have to have a dress removed by a stranger, I should at least get to do something I enjoy. I should at least get to see that happy look on their faces.

Get a little more love.

And so that's what I do.

I actually do it.

Wanna play?

From now on, the answer is always yes.

I drop whatever I am doing and I go to my children and I play.

It's a rule. No. I've made it more than a rule. I've made it law. Canon. Text. It's a religion. There's a strict obedience to it. Something that I practice. With fervor.

Imperfectly.

But faithfully.

Unquestioningly.

Making it such a steadfast rule allows me to peel away some of the work pressure I put on myself. To know that I "don't have a choice" means that I don't feel any guilt stepping away from my workaholic tendencies. I feel no remorse dumping my purse and coat on the floor just as I'm walking out the door to head to the office when I hear those two magic words—*wanna play*? Those two words have me out of my shoes and sitting at the tiny pink tea table coloring a bunny or playing with the unfortunate one-eyed baby doll or staring at lizards in the garden in an instant.

It's hard to nail down a tween—if you have one, you know what I mean. I vividly remember being twelve years old. I sometimes wonder how my parents allowed me to survive. At that age, the existence of one's parents is nothing more than an embarrassment. Clearly a twelve-year-old is never going to say "Wanna play?" But with Harper, I've learned to look for the words and signs that mean the same thing. If she wanders into my room in the evening and lies down on any piece of my furniture, I put down what I'm working on and give her my full attention. Sometimes that pays off. Sometimes it doesn't. But what I've come to understand is that letting her know my full attention is available is more important than anything else.

Also? I have discovered something about this tall, gangly

girl I love so much that sometimes she has to say "Please stop hugging me" so I will stop: I really *like* her.

She's *interesting.*

I'm discovering her. She's like an endless mystery. I can't wait to see how she's going to turn out.

It may be different for you. Your happy place. Your joy. The place where life feels more good than not good. It doesn't have to be kids. My producing partner Betsy Beers would tell me that for her that place is her dog. My friend Scott would probably tell me that for him it is spending time being creative. You might say it's being with your best friend. Your boyfriend, your girlfriend. A parent. A sibling. It's different for everyone. For some of you, it might even be work. And that, too, is valid.

This *Yes* is about giving yourself the permission to shift the focus of what is a priority from what's good for you over to what makes you feel good.

(Wait. Not heroin. Heroin is not your happy place.

Just cross all drugs off the list.

Are we clear? Okay.

Find a good happy place. A positive one.)

I have shifted my priorities. My job is still incredibly important. It's just that playing with my kids is now *more* important than my job.

In case the idea of doing this makes you nervous, makes you anxious, freaks you out? Makes you think I'm an idiot?

You might say, "That's all very nice for you, Shonda.

You're the boss at your job but I am a cashier so please tell me how I can turn my back on my job and still feed my family, stupid TV lady with your lace shoes and your diamonds. I hope your tiara squeezes your brains right out of your head."

I agree with you.

Whitney Houston. Curling iron. Solidarity.

But here's the thing that I hope helps. Here's the thing that I learned very quickly: nobody wants to spend that much time with me. Or with you. You know why?

You aren't Taylor Swift.

Or Curious George.

Or Rihanna.

Or the Muppets.

I mean that in a good way. A great way.

I mean that you can do this. I mean no matter how busy you are, how hectic your life is, you can probably pull this off in some way.

Emerson and Beckett only ever want to play with me for fifteen minutes or so before they lose interest and want to go do something else. It's an amazing fifteen minutes. But it's fifteen minutes. After fifteen minutes, I'm no one. If I'm not a grasshopper in the yard or a Popsicle or the Very Hungry Caterpillar, I may as well be a tree. Most of the time, Harper only ever wants to talk to me for fifteen minutes as well—sometimes less. I can pull off fifteen minutes . . . I can

TOTALLY pull off fifteen minutes of uninterrupted time even on my worst day.

Uninterrupted is the key: no cell phone, no laundry, no dinner, no anything. You have a busy life. You have to get dinner on the table. You have to make sure they get homework done. You have to force them to bathe. But you can do fifteen minutes.

While I was shocked to discover how little time this Yes to Play commitment really took and how easy it was to incorporate it into my daily life, it was about more than this. What was most difficult was what it forced me to face about myself.

I discovered that age-old cliché is true: people do what they like to do. I work because I like working—I am good at it, it works for me, it's my comfort zone. Knowing, facing the fact that I was more comfortable on a soundstage than on a swing set was incredibly difficult to *handle*. What kind of person is more comfortable working than relaxing? Well . . . me. So this Yes required me to change. It's a difficult challenge for a hard-working, straight-A, obsessive perfectionist to leap into a lifestyle practice that requires dropping everything to . . . *play*.

As I've said, my earliest memories were of imagining in the pantry. As I got older, I preferred the library to any other play space, the books inside to any other companion. When forced outdoors for fresh air and sunshine, I grabbed a book and stuffed it down the back of my pants to hide my contraband. Then I'd climb the willow tree in our backyard and read until my mother allowed me back in. Playing . . . ? I don't remember any real playing . . .

My nanny, Jenny McCarthy, watches all this unfold with solemn eyes. She watches me drop my bags and get down on the floor, awkward and stiff. She offers suggestions.

"You should play with the blocks."

"What if you all did some painting?"

Jenny McCarthy is quietly guiding me. Teaching me how to play. Teaching the stiff, introverted workaholic in me what play means for those outside the pantry doors, outside the library shelves. She's teaching me how to reach and connect with these little extroverts so different from me.

I feel like some kind of alien. Never before on this planet. Learning what this world is like. Jenny McCarthy is showing me how to live. Through these tiny karmic beings sent by the universe to help roll the rock away from the door of my cave and shove me into that bright beautiful sun.

And I am grateful.

We run around the yard. Up and back and up and back. We have thirty-second dance parties in the kitchen. We sing show tunes. We play with baby dolls and hand puppets and Fisher-Price farms.

It's the bubbles that do it.

I'm sitting in the backyard blowing an endless series of bubbles for the girls. The bubbles are filling the air; I'm on a roll, blowing as fast as I can to create a sea of bubbles all around their faces. They are squealing, popping bubbles and tasting bubbles and chasing bubbles. Beckett runs over and presses her sweaty body into me. She has that slight musky dirty kid smell. It always smells to me like . . .

"You smell like puppies!" I tell them.

And suddenly a painting is hung back on my wall:

My mother's in the backyard tending to her big round roses. The sun has just gone down. And my sister Sandie and I are racing around the backyard, each with a glass Mason jar. Trying to catch fireflies. Squealing and chasing fireflies, catching them, staring at them, our faces glowing in their light. Then, just when my mother calls for bedtime, we open the jars and release them into the night air.

"You smell like puppies," my mother laughs as she shoos us inside.

So now my memory stands corrected. I used to play. When I was this age. I played. I was happy. I liked it. I smelled like puppies. I was a puppy party.

I played.

I don't know why I ever stopped.

I suddenly find that I start asking *myself* the same question that the children ask me: *wanna play?*

Yes. Yes, I do.

But in order to do so, I know I have to make some real changes.

I make a rule that I will not work on Saturday or Sunday unless it's an emergency or unless the show is filming. I've been guilty of working straight through far too many weekends in order to "get ahead." There's no such thing. The work is always there in the morning.

I change the bottom of my email signature so that it now reads: **"<u>Please Note</u>: I will not engage in work emails after 7 pm or on weekends. IF I AM YOUR BOSS, MAY I SUGGEST: PUT DOWN YOUR PHONE."** And then I do what seems impossible: I *actually stop answering emails that arrive after seven p.m.* I have to turn off my phone to do it. But I do it. I have incredibly expert people working for me who run our sets. Learning to step back and let these people have the pleasure of doing their jobs without my peering over their shoulders has been great for them and for me both.

I make a vow to come home by six p.m. every night for dinner. If an issue is happening at work, I can find a way to come home from six p.m. to eight p.m. to be with the kids and then hop on my computer and work from home after that. Technology should be making it easier and easier for this to happen.

I'm not perfect at it.

In fact, I fail as often as I succeed. But what I know now is that this downtime is helping to relight that little spark inside, it's helping my creativity and in the long run helping me tell the stories my work needs me to tell. I give myself permission to view this downtime as essential. It's hard to do. It's hard to feel like I deserve any time to replenish the well when I know everyone else is working hard too. Except once again, there's Delorse in my kitchen:

"Shonda, what happens when you get sick? What happened that time you threw your back out? That time you had the flu?"

We don't like to talk about it at work. It's like tempting fate. But Delorse means when I go down, the shows go down. If I go down, eventually things in Shondaland come to a halt. Because of that track laying that has to happen. The stories originate with my brain. And if they can't come out of my brain, no one can even begin to lay track. And if the track can't be laid, the train cannot roll. It's the same with Kerry Washington, Viola Davis, Ellen Pompeo—if one of them goes down, so goes a show. The cameras can't roll without them. It makes it incredibly essential to keep in good shape.

Ellen, who seems to have more stamina and determination than anyone I've ever seen, once said that making twenty-four episodes of network television is like running a marathon twenty-four times. Since season one, she has treated herself like an athlete in training. Ellen believes that to do her job well, she needs to take care of herself—inside and out. Ellen's approach becomes my inspiration. I decide maybe it's time I started thinking the same way about my job.

For me, that means that if track is going to be laid, I need some time to play.

Wanna play?

Home by six. No phones after seven. Try not to work weekends.

Then I expand it.

Wanna play?

I use it as a way of allowing myself to seek comforts I would not normally allow. "Wanna play?" starts to become a shorthand for indulging myself in ways I'd forgotten about.

Manicures? Pedicures?

Wanna play? YES.

Browse for hours in an actual bookstore on a Saturday afternoon when the kids are on a playdate?

Wanna play? YES.

A long bath with some Aretha Franklin blaring loud enough that no one can hear me singing?

Wanna play? HELL YES.

A glass of wine and a square of chocolate and fifteen minutes of guiltless silence with my door closed?

Wanna play? Please keep your voice down, but . . . yes.

Fifteen minutes, I say. What could be wrong with giving myself my full attention for just fifteen minutes?

Turns out?

Nothing.

The more I play, the happier I am at work. The happier I

am at work, the more relaxed I become. The more relaxed I become, the happier I am at home. And the better I get at the playtime I have with the kids.

It's really just love.

We could all use a little more love. A lot more love.

For the kids. For me.

This is the best YES.

Wanna play?

Yes to My Body

Here's a thing I maybe forgot to mention.

When I decide to begin my Year of Yes?

That night I decide I am going to start saying yes to the things that scare me? That night I told you about when I am lying on the sofa with a glass of wine staring at my Christmas tree?

I am fat.

I'm not cutely chubby. Or nicely plus-size.

I am not round in my rump.

I don't have junk in my trunk.

I'm not voluptuous.

I'm not going pa-*pow* and ba-*bam* in all the right places.

I'm not working my curves the way I did in college.

If I was, you can bet I would be wearing something cute and tight and daring you to say something about it.

But that is not what is going on.

No.

I am fat.

I am obese.

I am the biggest I have ever been in my entire life.

I am so fat that I am uncomfortable in my own skin. So fat that I'm having the surreal experience of catching a glimpse of myself in a mirror and wondering with genuine confusion, "Who is that?" It actually takes a few seconds for my brain to catch up, for me to realize, with shock, that I am looking at my own reflection. That stranger is me. I am staring at myself encased in many, many extra pounds of fat. So many I'm afraid to get on a scale.

I am *massive*.

But that's not the thing.

I *am* massive.

But more important . . .

. . . I *feel* massive.

Which *is* the thing.

Look. I will not be told what size to be. I do not care about anyone else's judgment about my body. I am not interested in anyone else's ideas of what I'm supposed to look like.

I believe everyone's body is theirs and everyone has a right to love their body in whatever size and shape and package it comes in. I will fight for anyone's right to do so. I will kick ass and take names if I have to. Your body is yours. My body is mine. No one's body is up for comment. No matter how small, how large, how curvy, how flat. If you love you, then I love you.

But this is not about loving me.

I don't FEEL good.

And while part of me means it emotionally, I mostly mean it physically.

I don't FEEL GOOD.

My knees hurt. My joints hurt. I discover that the reason I am so exhausted all the time is because I have sleep apnea. I am now on high blood pressure medication.

I can't get comfortable.

I can't touch my toes.

My toes are *untouchable*.

I need to eat a piece of cake to cope with this discovery.

I am a mess.

I do not know how this has happened.

Except I do.

Remember that genetic Powerball lottery the women in my family have won? The one that means we will never look older than a pack of terribly tired teenagers? It seems there's also a metabolic SuperLotto that had the winning numbers—but only for HALF the women in my family. So my sisters Delorse and Sandie have the great luck of not only looking fourteen years old but also being able to eat half a cow in one sitting and never look larger than, well, a FOURTEEN-YEAR-OLD. I, on the other hand, did not draw those numbers. Fat runs toward me and jumps up onto my body and clings there. Like it knows that it has found a home. Like it wants to be with its people.

I've battled my weight my entire life. It always seemed unfair. It was always a horrible struggle. And after a while, I decided that struggling was not worth it. So I stopped battling. I stopped starving myself. And I settled in at what seemed like a not too heavy but not skinny weight. Plus-size. Juicy. Curvy. Definitely cute. Great booty. I was healthy. I was working out. I wasn't thinking too much about my body anyway.

And then . . . I lost control of the wheel.

Don't ask me exactly when. I'm not sure.

But I know it coincided with my slowly closing all the doors of my life. Saying no to things. Shutting down.

And here's the thing. It didn't really feel like that was what was happening.

I mean, I had a lot going on.

I had some excellent excuses for letting go of that wheel.

I decided to freeze my eggs. Like, the ones inside my body. Babies. Yes! The miracle of life. In order to freeze your eggs, you have to inject yourself with some hormones. Now, if you are a naturally thin person, you seem to stay thin. If you are me . . . not so much.

Then out of nowhere, I had a minor surgery. Which made me go, "I better stop all of this working out. And maybe lie down here on this sofa for a bit to recuperate."

Um, the surgery was on my eye.

So?

What's your point?

It doesn't matter that the surgery was on my eye. My EYE needed to recuperate. But when my eye was better, that sofa kind of needed me. It didn't seem *that* important to get back up. Plus, there was some good TV on.

Oh, yes. TV. I had a job. *Grey's Anatomy.* Then I had two jobs. I added *Private Practice.* Then I had three jobs. I added *Scandal* on top of those shows. And then just as I said good-bye to *Private Practice*, we began producing *How to Get Away with Murder.* And the more shows I had, the more I could be found at my desk or on a sofa in an editing room. The more I could be found sitting on my butt. The more I sat, the less I moved.

The less I moved?

Don't make me say it . . .

And the shows were doing so well. Which was like some kind of cruel joke. If something had failed, the irony was that I would have had the time to take myself to the gym. I would have had the time to get some rest. I would have had the time to take care of myself. At least, that's the story I told myself. But nothing got canceled. I was succeeding. I was doing more than succeeding.

It's incredibly rare for a television drama to run even three seasons, and by this point, the shows I'd created had all gone at least five.

Shondaland was a brand now. The studio expected us to produce more shows. The network expected me to maintain the quality of the ones currently on the air. Now I owned an entire night of the most expensive real estate on television. TGIT had taken over social media. Everyone around me seemed invested. Very invested. I started having nightmares about getting canceled.

Delorse and Jenny McCarthy fussed over me, worrying that my creativity would be affected by stress. They didn't understand—my creativity was the one place I never felt stress. Creating worlds, characters, stories has always been where I am most at ease. With the empty whiteboard of an episode before me, I slip into a zone of calm confidence. I feel the *hum*. Making television for me is . . . blissful. I can make stuff up the way other people can sing—I have simply always been able to hit all the notes. At its core, a TV show is just a bigger pantry. So I wasn't worried about writing the shows or making the shows.

I was worried about rising expectations. I was worried about the stakes.

Oh, yeah. Maybe I should mention: there are stakes, and man oh man, are they *high*.

As the shows got more popular, I was acutely, painfully aware of what was at stake. I smiled, refused to answer the question, pretended I didn't know what reporters were asking me about when they asked about race. But you can't be raised black in America and *not* know.

This wasn't just my shot. It was *ours*.

I had to do everything right. I had to keep it all afloat. I had to run to the top of the mountain. I could not rest, I could not fall, I could not stumble, I could not quit. Failing to reach the summit was not an option. Failing would be bigger than just me. Blowing it would reverberate for decades to come. With *Grey's Anatomy*, it would mean that giving an African-American woman her own show with a cast that looked like the real world was a mistake. I proved it wasn't.

The stakes got even higher for *Scandal*. If the first network drama with an African-American leading lady in thirty-seven years didn't find an audience, who knows how long it would take for another to come along? Failure meant two generations of actresses might have to wait for another chance to be seen as more than a sidekick.

I am what I have come to call an F.O.D.—a First. Only. Different. We are a very select club, but there are more of us out there than you'd think. We know one another on sight.

We all have that same weary look in our eyes. The one that wishes people would stop thinking it remarkable that we can be great at what we do while black, while Asian, while a woman, while Latino, while gay, while a paraplegic, while deaf. But when you are an F.O.D., you are saddled with that burden of extra responsibility—whether you want it or not.

When I made my first television show, I did something I felt was perfectly normal: in the twenty-first century, I made the world of the show look the way the world looks. I filled it with people of all hues, genders, backgrounds and sexual orientations. And then I did the most obvious thing possible: *I wrote all of them as if they were . . . people.* People of color live three-dimensional lives, have love stories and are not funny sidekicks, clichés or criminals. Women are the heroes, the villains, the badasses, the big dogs. This, I was told over and over, was trailblazing and brave.

I hope you have your left eyebrow raised too, dear reader. Because—girl, please. But I was doing a thing that the suits had said could not be done on TV. And America was proving them wrong by watching. We were literally changing the *face* of television. I was not about to make a mistake *now.* You don't get second chances.

Not when you're an F.O.D.

Second chances are for future generations. That is what you are building when you are an F.O.D. Second chances for the ones who come behind you.

As Papa Pope told his daughter Olivia: "You have to be twice as good to get half as much . . ."

I didn't want half. I wanted it all. And so I worked four times as hard.

I never wanted to have to look at myself in the mirror and say that I didn't try as hard as I could to make these shows work. That I didn't give 100 percent to leave a legacy for my daughters and for all the young women of color out there who wondered what was possible. It irritated me *to my core* that we live in an era of ignorance great enough that it was still necessary for me to be a role model, but that didn't change the fact that I was one.

I got into the habit of working as hard as I could all the time. My life revolved around work. And outside of work, I took the path of least resistance. I didn't have the energy for difficult conversations or arguments. So I smiled and let people get away with treating me however they wanted. And that only made me yearn to be back in the office. Where I was in charge. Where I was the boss. Where people were too respectful or kind or happy or afraid to treat me like crap.

Because I worked so much, I found myself constantly tired. In the early days of *Grey's*, I said no to so many invitations that people actually stopped asking me. I began to have a reputation as someone who did not socialize with work people outside of work. In reality, I didn't socialize with *any-*

one outside of work. My larger circle of friends also didn't understand; there were whispers I'd abandoned them for a glamorous Hollywood life filled with parties and famous friends. I would have laughed at this, but I was just too tired. I'd get an angry email about a missed birthday and would be asleep face-first on my keyboard before I could craft an apologetic response. Finally I just . . . gave up. My friends self-selected down to a smaller core group. I stayed home more. And spent more time working. More time alone. More time hiding.

Losing yourself does not happen all at once. Losing yourself happens one *no* at a time. No to going out tonight. No to catching up with that old college roommate. No to attending that party. No to going on a vacation. No to making a new friend. Losing yourself happens one pound at a time.

The more I worked, the more stressed I was. The more stressed I was, the more I ate.

I knew things were getting out of hand. As I started to feel more uncomfortable. As I started to feel more tired. As the jeans got tighter and tighter. When I went up size after size. When I needed the largest-size clothing in the plus-size shop.

And yet.

I was ambivalent about so much of it. The feminist in me didn't want to have the discussion with myself. I resented the need to talk about weight. It felt as though I was judging myself on how I looked. It felt shallow. It felt misogynistic.

It felt . . . traitorous to care.

My body is just the container I carry my brain around in.

I started saying that back in college when the frat guys would make dirty comments about my boobs. And I used this tone. A tone that said, *God, how dumb are you?*

But I had to say it to them a lot. To make them know that I should be invisible to them. To make them stop looking.

And now I was saying it to myself a lot. To make me invisible to myself.

My body is just the container I carry my brain around in.

I said it while I ate cartons of ice cream.

I said it while I ate whole pizzas.

I said it while I enjoyed mac and cheese with bacon in it. You heard me. *Bacon* in it. I ate anything that had bacon in it. Or was wrapped in bacon. One meat wrapped in another meat clearly proved the universe was unfolding exactly as it should.

My body is just the container full of bacon that I carry my brain around in.

And maybe it is. Maybe it is just the container I carry my brain around in.

But so is a car. And if the car is broken down and busted, my brain isn't going anywhere. Same goes for my container.

I felt . . . old. Not "I'm old and I like to lie" old.

Old.

"Stop participating in the world" old.

"Sit in a chair and watch the world go by" old.

What an extraordinary waste of a life.

But what a tasty human veal . . .

I think no one is noticing. I think no one sees. I think the fact that I have doubled in size may not be that noticeable. Because I don't really notice it. It's happened so gradually. I am invisible to myself. I think I am maybe invisible to everyone.

I am not.

People tried to be tactfully helpful. People said things to me like, "Endorphins make you feel good."

So does chocolate cake, fool.

Betsy Beers, whom I love and adore and would honestly slay a dragon for (or at least kill a spider for), once said, "You just have to train yourself to love salads."

I did not speak to her for several days. Who *trains themselves to love salads?*

What kind of sicko trains themselves to love salads?! I could also train myself to love the taste of gravel. Or cow crap. But why? I don't hate myself.

I hired a trainer. And then I promptly fired him because he said, "Nothing tastes as good as thin feels!"

He clichéd at me.

He clichéd at me in a perky, condescending tone.

"Nothing tastes as good as thin feels!"

Who says that to a fat woman? Seriously? WHO SAYS THAT? Because clearly, a) you have never had barbecue ribs, and b) shut your stupid mouth.

Being tasty veal is not something I'm happy about. Even veal does not want to be veal. Veal wants to be rescued by PETA. I start to long to be rescued as well.

I get on a plane to New York. I'm a fancy TV writer. So I have a first-class ticket, a big first-class comfy seat. I settle in, shoes off, pull out my book, grab the seat belt and—

Well, it's gotta be broken.

It's BROKEN, right?

I HAVE A BROKEN SEAT BELT.

Right? RIGHT?

I do not have a broken seat belt.

I am literally too fat for a first-class airplane seat belt. I am Violet Beauregarde blowing up like a giant blueberry in Willy Wonka's factory. I'm the thing that ate Gilbert's grape. Poke me with a pin and I am going to pop like a balloon.

I freaking wish.

At least it would mean I wouldn't be a passenger on this plane.

The humiliation is starting to make me sweat. A sweaty Shonda is not a pretty Shonda. A sweaty Shonda is a short leap away from a hideous troll-like Shonda.

I decide that I have two choices: I can ask the flight attendant for the seat belt extender, or I can go without a seat belt, thus ensuring that karma will crash the plane and I will plummet to my death, taking hundreds of innocent seat-belt-wearing, law-abiding people with me.

You know me pretty well by now, gentle reader. What do you think I do?

Do you think I act like an adult, like a grown-ass woman who ate herself here? Do I hit that button to summon the flight attendant? Do I speak to the flight attendant in a clear and calm voice, carefully enunciating each word so everyone in the first-class cabin is sure to hear what the sweaty girl in seat 5A has to say?

"Excuse me, but it has just come to my attention that I am now way too fat for this big giant first-class airplane seat belt. May I have the very same seat belt extender that I used to smirk to myself about while thinking superior thoughts? MAY? I? PLEASE?"

Really? Me?

Please.

No.

You know me by now. You *know* I don't do that.

I choose death.

I choose death by fat and by karma and because *Catholicism don't quit*, I bravely choose to deal with the hellfire and damnation that will follow forever after as punishment for taking the rest of the plane's passengers down with me.

I toss my sweater over my lap to hide the lack of seat belt, give an apologetic smile to the man in the suit across the aisle, shut my eyes tight and wait for the painful death that is to come.

I don't die.

I'm not dead.

Hot *damn*, I'm a narcissist—did I seriously expect karma to take down a whole planeload of people because my ass got too fat and my ego got too big to admit it?

I'm alive.

But I immediately start to imagine myself dead. Imagine myself being embalmed. Imagine myself being worked on in a funeral home. Some lady putting makeup on my dead fat face. I think of the extra-large coffin. The enormous tent my sisters will have to buy to give to the funeral director to dress me in.

It sounds funny.

Not to me.

Nothing about this is funny to me.

I have two toddlers and a twelve-year-old.

What the *hell* have I been doing to myself?

I find myself wondering, "How do I *yes* this one?"

The Year of Yes, I realize, has become a snowball rolling down a hill. Each yes rolls into the next into the next and the snowball is growing and growing and growing. Every yes changes something in me. Every yes is a bit more transformative. Every yes sparks some new phase of evolution.